Suffolk Coun

CW00400767

Libraries

Join the WAAF in '41

6
)17

ASO M.I. Park, January 1943

Join the WAAF in '41

M. IRENE PARK

Copyright © M. Irene Park, 2002

First published in 2002 on behalf of the author
by Scotforth Books,
Carnegie House,
Chatsworth Road,
Lancaster LA1 4SL,
England
Tel: +44(0)1524 840111
Fax: +44(0)1524 840222
email: carnegie@provider.co.uk
Publishing and book sales: www.carnegiepub.co.uk
Book production: www.wooof.net

British Library Cataloguing-in-Publication data
A catalogue record for this book is available from the British Library

ISBN 1-904244-14-9

Typeset in Bell 12 on 14 by Carnegie Publishing
Printed and bound in the UK by Bookcraft, Midsommer Norton

To the many disabled in war, mentally and physically, and to the 'foundations' which care for them, among whom all proceeds will be shared

Contents

Illustrations

* Assistant Section Officer – lowest commissioned rank
✝ Aircraftwoman 2 – lowest non-commissioned rank

Preface

I ALWAYS KNEW that my mother found it difficult to throw out family letters, but just how difficult I realised not long ago when I came across some of my own, written during the Second World War. On reading them, I became completely absorbed and it occurred to me that the next generation in the family might find interest and/or amusement in reminiscences of those days. One thing led to another, and here they are for what they are worth.

The war is past history now, but for those involved it was a world of its own and even at this distance one's recollections are clear as clear – like seeing them through the 'wrong' end of a telescope.

M. Irene Park
Moffat, Scotland.

Chapter One

'LEFT LEFT ... LEFT RIGHT LEFT ... left ... left ... left right left. *Pick up those feet.* Left ... left ...' The scraping noise went on to my right, and out of the corner of my eye I could see a small, slight figure in a black coat, leaning forward at an angle of about 45°, dragging along behind her the blackest, heaviest pair of shoes imaginable (and about as far removed as possible from her accustomed light high heels). This was Mary, the saving grace those first few desperate days.

That night, with lights out, the hut in total darkness and the only sound a stifled sob here and there, footsteps could be heard in the distance. As they came near, a small Glasgow voice piped up, in time with the steps: 'Left ... left ... left right left ... Left ... left ... left right left ... *Pick up those feet ...*' It was perfect, and everyone burst out laughing. Afterwards there was silence. The tension had gone.

The Equipment Section stocked uniforms of most shapes and sizes but they had not been able to produce one for Mary Docherty. She was minute. All they had been able to provide for her that first day were stockings and shoes (the afore-mentioned 'beetle crushers'), hence her parading in her own 'civvy' coat while the rest of us sported very new Air Force-blue uniform, WAAF. And when they did produce one for her, she was furious. Mary, it transpired, was in mourning – her young husband had been lost at sea not long before – but she was not to be allowed to wear mourning in any shape or form – no black armband, no black triangle, nothing. 'Jeest,' she muttered, tossing her head, 'if the King's deed.'

It was in fact quite difficult to follow all that she said, but she kept bringing her mother into it. She, we gathered, had been adamant about the wearing of mourning, and Mary had certainly arrived at the depot in deepest black from head to foot. 'If no,' she kept repeating, 'she'll no let me ower the door or ben the hoose!' By this time the entire hut had become embroiled, but as a fellow-Scot I felt somehow particularly involved/responsible. Then my eye lighted on someone's tie. 'But,' I said quietly, hopefully, 'we're in RAF uniform now, with black ties, and black ties always indicate mourning.' This was met with universal agreement and approval – relief all round.*

Another in our ranks had a fearful drill problem of a different kind – Phyllis from South Wales. Probably the only child of elderly parents, poor Phyllis took life very seriously. She was all right at drill when we were just marching along in silence, became agitated to a degree when the instructor shouted the by-now familiar 'Left ... left ... etc.,' but when he called out, 'Swing those arms ... higher ... *higher*,' one could sense mounting panic. Up would go her right arm with her right leg, her left with her left. As they went even higher, her balance would begin to go ...

With this, and Mary dragging her anchors, and the inevitable few who could never distinguish right from left so that on the command 'Right wheel' or 'Left wheel', some in the outer rank would go sailing off across the parade-ground on their own while others bumped into their neighbours, and the fact that we were weary in the extreme (the result of little sleep and having to get up in what seemed to be the middle of the night – going from hut to dreaded ablution block in brilliant moonlight), the rest of us were all but hysterical. What it was like for the instructors I can't imagine – probably a stock threat to RAF

---

* Mary had joined up as a batwoman, and must have enlivened many a household, many a life. She was irrepressible.

sergeants: 'If... you'll be posted to one of the WAAF depots to drill recruits.'

All this was taking place 'somewhere in England', in fact Innsworth, Gloucester, in November 1941, a stage in the Second World War when recruitment, certainly in the WAAF, was reaching a peak – something which was to have a direct bearing on my WAAF career. The number of trades open to WAAF by then was over 50 (compared with the five when the Women's Auxiliary Air Force was officially formed, in June 1939) and entrants were pouring in.

I had joined up as a Clerk, Special Duties – Clerk S. D. – plotter. By then, however, the Battle of Britain was over, jobs relating to defence were not required to the extent that they had been, and in view of this rapid rise in intake, anyone armed with the remotest degree of leadership was being steered into what in civilian life would be regarded as welfare; or so it seemed. As one of the others, similarly diverted from her chosen trade, put it, 'Obviously anyone who had been a Girl Guide or prefect at school ...'. And so I became ACW2 Park, Admin.

We were only at the depot for a matter of days but during the time I did manage to locate the friend of a friend who, I had discovered, was joining up on the same day. I did this by careful scrutiny during a roll-call and follow-up later. (We went our separate ways after initial training but were to come face to face in quite amusing circumstances the following summer!) In addition to meeting Stella, and the saga of Mary D., four things come vividly to mind when I think of Gloucester as depot. (I add that because I was to visit it again on a course.)

One was the cook-house, which we entered armed with our 'irons' (knife, fork and spoon), where we ate as quickly as possible from the one plate provided, and hopefully before the various elements met in the middle – jam perhaps from one side and kidneys floating across from the other. One of the things I found most difficult to take was already-sweetened tea – no choice –

dispensed from a giant urn, and to be drunk out of the biggest mugs ever. (My mug was to feature in quite an occasion/ celebration some time later, on a Bomber Station, but that is jumping ahead.) One's implements were 'washed' by being dipped in a tub of rather murky-looking water as we walked out. The mind boggles at the level of hygiene here, but having said that, the standard of health generally was extremely high. No doubt any germs would have been hard put to it to survive in the conditions prevailing!

Another never-to-be-forgotten feature of the depot was the so-called ablution block, and I shiver/shudder at the very thought of those lines of basins and loos, the concrete floor, the few – very few – baths but ne'er a plug to be seen. As someone said, they were probably pinched, as possession of a plug would make a bath possible – certainly easier – though why anyone should have wanted to have a bath ... the very sight of them and those soggy duckboards alongside ...

The issue of uniform is another. Set out on countless tables in the Equipment Section were stacks of every garment to be issued – caps, bras, the lot – and a WAAF behind each, dishing them out. As we walked along, we would be scrutinised, a garment deemed to be the right size, or as near as, handed over and we would move on, ending up with quite a pile. Then it was off to our hut and a total switch from our 'civvies' (so-called) to WAAF uniform, the former consigned to the empty suitcases which we had taken with us for the purpose, and duly sent home.

The fourth feature or procedure which comes to mind is our first Church Parade, and the sermon at the service. We were divided up: Jews, Roman Catholics, Church of England, and the rest – referred to as Jews, RCs, C. of E., and ODs (other denominations). This last-named seemed to me to be quite inevitable. After all there is a limit to the number designated – Methodists, Church of Scotland, Baptist, Congregational, etc. –

but some who were members of our old-established Church of Scotland were quite irate, considering it very demeaning to be lumped together or counted in as one of 'the rest', miscellaneous, whatever. What intrigued me about that Church parade was the fact that the OD group proved to be almost entirely Church of Scotland, and we were almost without exception to pattern – medium height, plumpish, reddish hair. Mention of this – colour of hair – produced an interesting comment when I remarked on it to someone years later – 'You don't think that WAAF uniform attracted that particular colouring?' It had certainly never occurred to me, and I don't think so. Perhaps north of the 'tartan curtain' we are just more of a type than we realise.

It was around Armistice time (now Remembrance Day) and no doubt part of the padre's sermon would have been devoted to remembrance and thanksgiving but what I remember most about it were the text and his interpretation of it. Unfortunately I have never been able to find the actual text, so cannot quote it word for word, but it was from the Old Testament – almost certainly Psalms – about coming up to the Lord 'in the morning', which was interpreted as the morning of life, i.e. youth, and the importance thereof.

And so to Morecambe, by special train – a whole trainload of WAAFs ...

There we were divided up into small groups (I was in one of about eight) and taken to private billets – mainly peacetime guesthouses – but although it was more like home than huts such as we had lived in at the depot, this was for many the most trying time. The novelty, or shock, had worn off, and I personally went through a period of real homesickness there. For one thing, I yearned to be on my own, even just occasionally, but the odd occasions on which I did succeed were not a great success. One was the occasional foray out and about between return to billet after our day's work and our high tea. I can recall it as though it were yesterday – wandering around, gnawing a carrot. We were nearly always hungry, fruit was very scarce if not actually unobtainable; sweets were rationed, and strictly so, and I remember the sight of a family in a lighted room never failed to reduce me to tears. I recalled this recently when an Australian friend told how in her childhood, curtains were never drawn, her mother being of the opinion that the sight of a large happy family might cheer a passer-by. I agree that is as it should be. I guess I just wasn't a big enough passer-by.

A feature of private billets was that one was at the mercy of one's landlady and we had chanced on the original of all the stories about seaside landladies. For example, for an evening cup of tea, which was an extra, she charged us 1½d. – even in canteens it was 1d. – and we had to enter the house by the back door, leaving our shoes in the scullery just inside, and it is that scullery, in Marine Road, that was the scene of one of my more memorable episodes in Morecambe. This was my first turn on potato-peeling duty. We did this in turn, in twos. (I discovered later that we need not have done this, but at that time we obeyed orders pretty automatically, and Mrs. H. would have taken a bit of opposing at the best of times!)

Not the most domesticated of animals, when potato-peeling (or indeed anything to do with cooking) was the order of the day at home, I would tend to be missing, or just not around – outside somewhere, chopping sticks, or making something, or helping in the garden. In fact, truth to tell, I had never peeled a potato in my life, and here I was – potato duty and no way out. Fortunately – and this was the saving of me – the scullery was very dimly lit, and there I sat, very confident-looking (I hoped), chatting away to my opposite number in front of a giant bucket of potatoes, knife in hand (no nice slick peeler as now) and dipping my potato in and out of the water about as often as she was fishing out a new one, hoping that she thought I

6

was doing the same. (There was just one bucket – fortunately – and one large rinse at the end.) It is one thing to retain one's individuality, quite another to seem to be different in a situation like this. To my relief I got away with it – I think. Her only comment was, 'It seems to be taking a hell of a long time tonight.'

Morecambe certainly had it moments. Another I remember vividly. The various units, sections, were spread about in the town – where gas drill was held, lecture rooms, medical unit, etc. and we marched always from A to B in squads. On this occasion I found myself in charge of my squad, marching along the front – a lovely day, quite enjoying it now that I had had some experience (about a week probably by then), a burgeoning pride in the Service, our Service, as people watched us go by, head held high, arms a-swinging. Alas, head was held too high and I failed to see a hole in the road. Down I went, head over heels, and when I collected myself I could see my cap bowling merrily along in the gutter, and my squad, in true Service tradition, marching briskly straight ahead, no order having been given – no right or left wheel, no 'halt' – they were out of earshot – and about to disappear under a bus. Fortunately the only casualty was my dignity, or pride.

I mentioned gas drill; it was very much part of our training, our schedule. By then – towards the end of 1941 – most civilians had given up carrying gas masks, but the possibility of the use of gas by the Germans was taken very seriously by the powers that be, and in addition to lectures about the various kinds – one, I remember, smelled like musty hay – phosgene? – we were actually shut in a gas-filled room, wearing our respirators, to give us confidence in them. Lectures took up a lot of our time, on various subjects, but my recollection is of hygiene and more hygiene – so-called. These were necessary, very necessary, no doubt but I must say one wondered if the die-hards would not just continue in their own sweet way, VD or no VD, and the inhibited close their ears as soon as this aspect of the subject was announced or even hinted at. In fact, judging by what I was to hear later, they should have gone right back to basics – the birds and the bees …!

I was to discover, from Admin officers mainly, but also from one rather shattered adjutant (RAF) how many WAAF there were with no knowledge of sex whatsoever – daughters no doubt of mothers brought up in ignorance in Victorian days and who did not see fit to enlighten their daughters either. Certainly ignorance or innocence was pleaded in cases where it was far from the truth, but time and again it was true, the odd one amazed when told she was pregnant – no idea. I remember being told about one, without any idea, being at work in the cookhouse until practically the last minute before the baby was born, or as it was told to me, rather more dramatically, 'she nearly had it on the hotplate'!

The adjutant referred to had been confronted by a somewhat desperate WAAF. She had done the right thing, i.e. reported to the WAAF officer in charge, to confess that she was pregnant but had been dismissed with – 'You can't be; you're not married,' and she had then reported to him.

Another, perhaps more understandable example: WAAF quarters were generally self-contained and clearly designated on Stations, and on this particular occasion the Flight-Sergeant WAAF was reporting to the WAAF Officer in charge that somehow a brilliant red light had been fixed up at the main entrance to the WAAF quarters. To her astonishment, and dismay, she was met with a blank look, and 'So …?' – the idea of red-light districts totally meaningless.

While on this subject I am taken back to a comment put to me in hushed tones in that hut in those never-to-be-forgotten early days at Innsworth. We were a real odd mixture but two seemed different and kept very much to themselves – young, attractive, and with few possessions – very little baggage. None of us had much but they seemed to have none. Someone said quietly and I am sure innocently, thinking of them as possibly having come to the depot straight from work as it were – hadn't gone home to collect the odd thing: 'Those two girls – d'you think they've just come in off the street?' I was somewhat nonplussed but we were moving around at the time and we went our separate ways. Then another came up to me – a rather more worldly one – and said; 'I couldn't help hearing that, about those two, but I thought that being a prostitute was a reserved occupation.' I knew of course that that applied to certain jobs or professions – doctors, nurses, farmers, etc. – but I have to admit I had never thought of that. Joining up had its moments – certainly in those bygone days!

But the *pièce-de-résistance* of my time in Morecambe was without doubt the occasion of my vaccination. I don't know if many found it difficult to cope with collar and tie – detached collar of course – but during my early days in uniform I had the greatest difficulty. This was partly because I had the idea that one had to attach the stud to one layer of shirt then one of collar, the other of shirt, etc. by which time my tie would have escaped. I had in fact to get up especially early to allow for this much-dreaded and time-consuming ritual.

When we arrived at the appointed place for vaccination, we were told to roll up our left shirt sleeve. I took off my

ACW2 in Morecambe, November 1941

jacket only to discover that my shirt, although it fitted perfectly when on, as it were, could not be rolled up, certainly not beyond my elbow. There was nothing for it; the shirt had to come off. That, I thought, means this so-and-so collar-and-tie business again – anything but that. So, thinking nothing of it, with considerable difficulty but eventual success, I managed to un-hitch my shirt from the studs and removed it only. When my turn came, I marched up to the M.O. (medical officer) with no cap on of course, no jacket *and no shirt* but with neatly done-up collar and tie. A strange expression came over his face and I thought, 'Goodness – what have I not done?'. We were very sensitive in the early days about doing the right thing, so I sprang to attention and threw up a terrific salute. (One never salutes without a cap on, but that was the least of it. I often wonder if he is still telling this story too!)

Inoculations presented no such problem – I must have had a more roomy shirt on that day, but I do remember people walking about with a needle sticking out of an arm, going from one M.O. to another to have another inoculation. Not many fainted, but it was the waggling needles that unnerved those who did.

Then came the great day when my posting came through. I was to report to a station in Suffolk not far from Newmarket – RAF Stradishall, Bomber Command, within 3 Group which took in a large part of East Anglia.

Chapter Two

I WAS TO BE THERE for just over a year and it was a year filled with incident and experience. We had the most wonderful Commanding Officer, and his influence permeated the station. His main interest must have been operations, flying, aircrew, and everything to do with all three – he was an outstanding pilot himself – but he concerned himself with everyone and everything under his command. I can say that from personal experience, having appeared on more than one occasion as escort of WAAF on charges, i.e. having been reported for some misdemeanour serious enough to be taken to the C.O. He was always fair, understanding, considerate – never harsh, overbearing or impatient and it was so nice, so gratifying to see someone like that rising to the top, for Group Captain Boyle was one day to become Chief of the Air Staff, and in due course Marshal of the Royal Air Force, Sir Dermot Boyle GCB KCVO KBE AFC.

When I arrived I was, as indicated earlier, Admin, and my duties to begin with consisted largely of escorting groups of new arrivals round the different sections. It may have been far from one's idea of 'playing one's part' but it served as a good introduction to a station, as I knew my way around in no time at all, and got to know the workings and the personnel in almost every section there.

There was one classic moment during one of these escort duties. I had taken a batch of new arrivals to a large room where booking in, signing on, etc., had to be done – the Orderly Room. There were RAF there too but a WAAF corporal seemed to rule the roost from a raised platform at one end. On this occasion the room was full of people and a buzz of conversation when the telephone rang. The afore-mentioned corporal, Corporal Jones – obviously very efficient, rather older than most of us – was concentrating on the filling-in of a form and continued to do so as she picked up the phone. There was a hushed silence as she did this, then a clear voice rang out. 'Ladies' underwear,' she said briskly. There was a pause, then as she blushed and collected herself, as it were, the conversation started up again, rather hurriedly. We all realised that she had just slipped back to 'civvy street' for the moment, but it was quite a moment while it lasted. Poor old Jonesy; she died not very long after, of cancer.

So far in my WAAF career I had lived in a hut – just two rows of beds, about thirty in all – and private billets (Gloucester and Morecambe respectively). At Stradishall I added to these airmen's married quarters (without the airmen!), a barrack block, with double-decker bunks, and what would be in peacetime officers' married quarters. I started off in the first of these, generally referred to as A.M.Q., and it was when returning there from a camp dance that I witnessed my first crash, or prang as it would be called then. It was a pitch black night and it happened right ahead of us, about a mile away. It was a Whitley. It had taken off, risen rather steeply, stalled, 'hit the deck' and burst into flames.

There were two immediate dangers – explosion of the bombs on board, and attracting the attention of any enemy snooper aircraft in the vicinity, but just what had happened then was enough for me. We stopped dead, then walked the rest of the way in silence. I had not been there very long then and had not got to know any aircrew, but when news got around as to which crew it was, I recognised the pilot's name – a name famous in Russia and Eastern Europe for generations – one of the Romanoffs. He was, I discovered, Czech. The rear-gunner had been thrown clear and was rushed to hospital not far away; all the others had been killed.

One thing I remember particularly about my time in A.M.Q. was the intense cold. The winter of 1941/42 was one of the coldest on record, and East Anglia can be as cold as anywhere when the wind is from an easterly direction – straight from the snow-clad Alps or from Siberia. We had a small coal fire in the downstairs room and a pathetically small allowance of coal, but as luck would have it, I had by then become friendly with a very nice airman – SP (Service Police) in fact, who proved to be a real friend in need. Knowing our predicament, he used to say to me every now and then, 'Leave your bucket at a certain place at a certain time and go back in about an hour;' and there, in the black-out, I would find our bucket filled with coal, and never did coal qualify more for the name 'black diamonds'. I am not sure where we stood morally in this. I don't think we stopped to think.

At one stage the cold was so intense that there was an almost complete freeze-up of pipes throughout the camp. There was no hot water in any of our usual wash places, and the situation was wretched if not pretty desperate when this same friend came to the rescue again, as far as I was concerned. 'There is hot water in the decontam,' he confided. 'The showers are OK,' and he told me exactly where and when to go. Now in our lectures on gas we had been informed/warned that although decontamination centres might sport separate entrances marked MEN and WOMEN, inside was one large open room where everyone would be stripped and hosed down as quickly as possible – no time for modesty – nothing like that.

All this was flickering in the back of my mind as I wended my way there at the appointed time, also how was I going to manage? I was going to have a shower – I knew that – and bath caps were not included in WAAF issue, and a bath cap I did not have. I did however have a tin hat which I had taken with me, and there unfolded another picture par excellence of me in my WAAF career – in a vast room, concrete floor, dimly lit, and under one of the shower fitments this figure clad in nothing but a tin hat, gyrating merrily (our tin hats had quite wide brims!) to the accompaniment of a variety of drip noises, not unlike a xylophone!

Though he obviously knew time and place, my friend, perfect gentleman that he was, did not put in an appearance. He merely inquired next day how it had gone. We were good friends, Les and I, and we played tennis quite a lot in the summer. He had a lovely turn of mind, and he loved drawing. In fact he became quite a famous cartoonist, and knowing that I enjoyed the odd bit of writing, he used to suggest that we combine our talents; I would do the writing and he the illustrations – the tin-hatted WAAF in the shower perhaps? Humorous drawings were his forte, and it is the comedy in life that one tends to remember fortunately. There was tragedy enough and more. However, we went our separate ways after Strad and I saw notice of his death in the press a number of years after the war.

I have another strange, rather eerie, memory of those AMQ days, associated with the darker side. It just happened that the particular WAAF friends I had made were without exception housed in OMQ (officers' married quarters in peacetime). I spent quite a lot of evenings with them there, and to return to my base directly I had to pass the mortuary, and this I just could not bring myself to do, in the dark. Countless times I would stand at the junction of the roads, telling myself not to be so stupid, not to let my imagination run away with me, etc. etc. etc., any and everything I levelled at myself, but in the end I always went the long way round – down by the M.T. (motor transport) section, along near the edge of the airfield and up again – three sides of a square. I was so afraid I might 'see' a group of aircrew come out, in flying kit, helmets hanging round their necks, parachutes slung over one shoulder, laughing and joking as they always seemed to do. The picture in my mind was so vivid, so acute, I felt that I could, just could have projected it and then seen it.

With so many of us in the same boat, as it were, one quickly became absorbed into life on a station and in no time at all I was a member of the choir and the dramatic society, both of which I enjoyed thoroughly. Later I was to be eternally grateful for my involvement with the latter as it was to save me from a posting which was not quite my cup of tea.

My enjoyment of being a member of the church choir was not merely the joy of singing, one of my favourite pastimes. It led to association with one of the nicest possible families – our padre, Squadron Leader 'Bill' Groom, his wife and children. They lived out, and they used to invite choir and friends to their house from time to time, keeping us in touch with a home and family atmosphere. They were kindness itself and I did keep in touch for a number of years. One just can't keep in touch with everyone, but one shared so much in wartime that when one does pick up the threads again, everything is just as when last we met.

We had a wonderful tenor in the choir and I remember towards the end of our first visit to their home, he quietly began to sing 'Bless this house', as beautifully as I have ever heard it sung, and from then on this became a regular feature of our visits, all together. The wish, or prayer – call it what you will – could not have been more sincere. We blessed their house indeed.

One visit I remember as though it took place yesterday. They kept geese and on this occasion the (quite large) goslings had escaped. We scattered to retrieve them and I captured one in a neighbouring field, connected with the rectory garden by a stile. The others, I noticed, were carrying theirs by the neck – no doubt the correct way – but I just couldn't (horrible feeling) and I was clutching mine round its body. All went well until we came to the stile, which I had to negotiate without help of hands. Whether in the process I squeezed my capture, or whether he was overcome by panic by then, I don't know, but the next thing I knew, the worst had happened and my skirt was covered! Mrs Groom, however, came to my rescue and I spent the evening in a skirt of hers (a tartan one, I remember) while mine was cleaned and dried as best we could in the time.

Although I was to keep up my interest in music (including singing, evenings of listening to records and, when there was absolutely no one else, playing the organ for services) and amateur dramatics throughout my time in the WAAF it was a great deal easier at this stage because as Admin I was not on night-duty or awkward shifts, and this made other activities possible too. I shall mention two that spring to mind, both, as it happens, with their grim side.

About this time – early 1942 – we were losing so many aircraft and therefore aircrew, the regular staff could hardly keep pace with what was called Committee of Adjustment work, i.e. the listing and despatch to next-of-kin of belongings of those killed or missing, and I helped with this at odd times – a heart-rending, but necessary task. It just happened that during this time the film *Dangerous Moonlight* was shown on the station and I found it almost unbearable when it came to the part where one hears them in the background listing belongings – kit etc. laid out, one calling, one writing down. It was horribly real. I may add that Rachmaninov's Piano Concerto No. 2 in C Minor recalls the feeling still. The Warsaw Concerto, the theme music of the film, was pretty close to it in every way.

The other rather trying duty was making tea for the crews on their return from ops. (operations) which could be at any time – 4, 5 or 6 a.m. depending on where the target had been, time of dawn, etc. Some were desperately white and shaky, some were positively bouncing (they might have been at a party), most were rather quiet. This cuppa was quite unofficial, pre-interrogation, and these occasions were among those I will never forget – not for them the short sharp fight more characteristic of Fighter Command. For these Bomber boys it was a long long flight, over enemy territory almost all the way there and back, and, for the pilot, the responsibility of his crew in whatever circumstances came their way.

For the extroverts it was a challenge, and the tougher of them quite revelled in it, e.g. our dramatic society producer, who was aircrew, 'If I'm not here at the beginning tomorrow evening, just carry on with Act Two ...' then on the evening of the morrow, in he would walk, rubbing his hands, saying 'Right ... where are we?' having been in hell let loose, over the Ruhr perhaps, a matter of hours before. For the very sensitive it must have been agony; one I can see still – ashen – and clutching and unclutching his hands.

One realised of course that sometimes it was a kind of bravado. I remember on one occasion hearing a pilot, who had just heard that a friend of his was now known to have been shot down, and killed, over Germany, say, 'He'll rot their crops.'; and I shall never forget the bantering dealt out to a WAAF officer friend, assistant Adjutant of a Flying Training Station, acting as Adjutant when he was on leave. A crash had occurred, both pilots had been killed, and she found herself responsible for funeral arrangements. As a rule overseas personnel were buried locally, others sent home and the RAF station nearest to their home took over the arrangements at that end. As it happened, one was from overseas (a New Zealander), the other British. 'Are you sure you've labelled them properly?' was one question with which she was faced. 'If,' his friend had gone on, 'you've sent Jimmy off labelled Harry H., he'll haunt you to the end of your days.' And another 'Have you got it properly organised at the other end? A pal of mine was left lying around in a Left-luggage office for days.' It sounds grim and callous stated like that, and I suppose it was really but it was the only way.

The Mess would be rather quiet for a day or two, but the gaps would be filled and life resumed. To quote a much-used phrase, one just 'pressed on regardless'. They would not be forgotten, just filed away, as it were.

I don't remember when I got my props, i.e. became an LACW (leading aircraft-woman – first step up, equivalent of an Army lance-corporal) but it must have been sometime in the spring (1942), for early in April I was sent off, with one or two other LACWs, on an NCO course – in Gloucester. As far as I can remember, it lasted for about a fortnight – perhaps a little more – and I quite enjoyed it. Even drill was quite fun, and now we were learning to take it, drilling our colleagues, that is, not recruits. I did not mention this when describing drill. in the context of our initial training, but quite an interesting feature of it was that it was used not only to get us accustomed to being marched around, on routine occasions but also, should the occasion arise, on big, formal parades (one to be included later, in Newmarket – stay tuned!) but it was also for the teaching of saluting, e.g., when and where.

Out on the parade-ground we would have been brought to a halt and then, to help us keep together, we would say out loud, as we saluted, 'One, two, three, down, the salute being held for the count of three; one, two, three, four; one, two, three, down, representing pause and second salute, one pause, two pause, left, right ... this being an about-turn and departure in the opposite direction. We were told that this would be the procedure if, for instance, we were delivering a letter to an officer in his or her room, the pause of one, two, three, four representing the handing-over of the missive. I mention this because on one famous occasion an Adjutant friend was treated to all of this, out loud, when a new WAAF entered his office and handed over a document. At first he thought she was raving mad, then it dawned – quite a moment!

This time, on our NCO Course, we were also learning such

things as when to give certain commands – Halt! for example to be called out while the right foot touches the ground so that they would step forward with the left and bring the right into it, coming to a halt – not as easy as it sounds, different commands demanding different timing, which reminds me of one poor officer-cadet when we were taking drill at OCTU, but that is still some way off.

Apart from revisiting a friend in Gloucester, the one who had kindly put me up the night before I reported at the depot, I seemed to do little apart from what was required of us on the course, but one thing I do remember, something which started as a rumour and then was proved to be true – the most unlikely person, we heard, was being failed – an LACW like the rest of us but the wife not only of a Group Captain but of one already famous, in fact almost a legend from his part in the Battle of Britain. Not only that, she would appear to have been very much of leadership material or whatever, very much so, perhaps too much. Anyhow we never knew what happened or why; we just all scattered, returning to our various units, and all of us who had gone from Strad (as RAF Stradishall was affectionately called) learnt in due course that we had passed; but the first few days after were filled with incident as far as I was concerned, all things I could well have done without.

The scene of the first was pay parade, my first since learning that I had become an NCO. I had sewn on my stripes, and incidentally was very proud of them. I had risen higher in the non-commissioned ranks than anyone else in the family! There I was, standing among my fellow-Corporals, in alphabetical order. The Flight-Sergeant had her name called out, then the ser-geants, and the rows of corporals were gradually disappearing. The name before mine was called out, and I was keyed up, ready to spring to attention, call out 'Sir, 168' (the last three of our service number) and go forward to the table, presided over by the Accounts Officer; but no, the next was not my name, nor the next, and to my horror the roll-call continued way beyond. What had happened was that the official notification of my promotion had not yet been logged in the Accounts Section and I was still listed among the LACWs. The others had been, and I had taken it for granted.

I stood and stood and stood, feeling more and more conspicuous as time went on, then the Accounts Officer must have become aware of a still figure before him, and he looked up. Slowly he looked me up and down, took in the stripes and very slowly he sat back in his chair. 'Good God,' he said. 'You, a corporal!' Then he sighed. 'Ah well,' he went on, 'cream will rise to the top.' He, Squadron Leader Baker, was quite a character – I had come to know him in some context or other – and he didn't mind at all this interruption. It broke the monotony of pay parade and I think he quite enjoyed it. Not so the WAAF officer presiding – I felt her eyes boring into me – a WAAF upsetting a parade, this familiarity etc. I just continued to look straight ahead and said not a word, and in the end was told to report to the Accounts Section later.

The next incident was a most tragi-sordid one. We had on the camp, and in the barrack-block, to which by this time I had moved, a most difficult character – Pat C., married at 16 to some real no-gooder in Liverpool's dockland, and currently an ACHGD (aircraft-hand general duties – the most unskilled trade). She had had a hopeless background, a hopeless life, she could stick at nothing and she just could not fit in. Our WAAF Officer in charge overall had been most understanding but nothing seemed to make much impression. Poor old Pat just felt that the world was against her, she was an out-and-out failure, and this particular evening she had gone out 'on the booze' and got blind drunk.

I was some way off – at the far end of one of the barrack-block rooms upstairs – when I became aware of the shuffling of feet, men's voices, intermittent groans, footsteps again, down by the entrance, and then quiet. Then the groaning started again and I heard someone coming up the stairs, calling out urgently, 'Corporal.' Obviously there had been some kind of crisis, and as I went down, I hoped and prayed that some more senior NCO would be around and take over. 'It's Pat,' someone said, 'Pat C.' and there she was lying on a bunk nearest the door, moaning and groaning, dribbling, clothes half-on, half-off. She had been found by one of our transports near a local pub, picked up and literally dumped. Apart from sending for someone from Sick Bay and covering her up, there was not a great deal I could do, but she did come round to an extent, and tried to say something. 'Don't,' she said in a slurred and shaky voice. 'Don't tell ...' At first I couldn't catch the name, then realised it was my own. Some of us had befriended her and she obviously felt she was letting us down.

To cut a long story short, she recovered, she was put on a charge, her case was gone into thoroughly (an example of our CO's wonderful approach and understanding) and she was put to work in Sick Bay – something she had always wanted to do, having been told, I must add, that she would be given this chance, but that if she were ever to appear on a charge again, it might be a different story. The transformation was nothing short of a miracle. She rose to it, she took pride in her appearance, she was thoroughly reliable, she worked hard, and she was happy for the first time in her life.

At first we dared not hope too much, but she kept it up, and after some months it seemed that all was well and set fair for the future. Then something was said to her – half-joking, half-serious – by a new NCO who did not know her history. She had omitted to do some quite small job and he had said, 'You know, you could be put on a charge for that.' One can imagine her state of mind. After all that had been done for her, and she appreciated it – there was no doubt of that – she just could not face the possibility, so she ran away. Service police rang up from Cambridge. They were holding an airwoman called Pat C. and they suspected that she was absent without leave. Now, of course, she would definitely be on a charge – a.w.l. (absent without leave) – or so she would think.

A small transport was sent from the station to collect her, and as they drove back, at fair speed along a good stretch of road, she pushed her WAAF escort away from her and jumped out of the back. By that time I was doing temporary duty at one of our satellite stations, and I will never forget our Flight Officer's face when she told me. They had taken Pat to a hospital in Newmarket but she died very soon after, and Mrs F. was visiting 'my' little unit on her way back from the hospital. Neither of us said much but I'm sure our thoughts were running along the same lines. Had we put too much responsibility on the girl? What else could we, should we have done? Looking back I still wonder, but I think really it was just bad luck the remark came when it did. Another six months and she might well have had confidence enough to cope with it, and all would have been well.

Such is the strain, the responsibility of an officer in charge, and as it happened, tragedy struck again within a week. A WAAF MT (motor transport) driver was killed – crushed against a hangar door by a large transport which had been parked close to it and was started up by someone who did not realise that it had been left in gear. He never left vehicles in gear in a position such as that, and he had not allowed for the possibility.

The third incident that greeted this brand-new corporal turned out all right in the end but gave me some moments of agony plus. Our AOC (Air Officer Commanding our Group) was leaving – he had been posted elsewhere – and on this particular day he was visiting our station to take his farewell. We were to be addressed in one of the hangars and the WAAF had been told to assemble outside the hangar opposite at a given time before, to be drawn up (marshalled into ranks/lines) and marched in. I happened to appear on the scene first – first of the Admin NCOs, having been near at the time, and a large rabble/gaggle of WAAF were there, just milling around, chattering hard. The appointed time was approaching, approached, and no sign of any of the others. Then a WAAF officer hove into view and I was seized with panic. In fact it is quite possible that my watch was fast and this WAAF officer early too but as far as I was concerned, the other officers would arrive any minute, then the CO and AOC himself, and there I was – the only admin NCO in sight.

I can recall the feeling now – panic stations, as we used to say. There were hundreds of WAAF milling round and talking, and I was sure that if I went out in front, I would call out to no avail, and then what? – but, something had to be done and done quickly. So, taking courage in both hands, I marched out to the space in front very suddenly, whirled round, swept a glance firmly, deliberately, from left to right and willed them to respond as I had never willed a mob before. Now whether that did it, or whether the sudden movement made them aware and they responded instinctively, I shall never know, but they literally swept into lines like waves *without my uttering a single word*. Just then the Flight-Sergeant, Sergeant and other corporals appeared round the corner and I melted thankfully into the throng.

The Dramatic Society I thoroughly enjoyed, and remember two plays particularly of those in which I took part: *Distinguished Gathering* by James Parish and *Rope* by Patrick Hamilton. The former was great fun, though it included some excruciating moments at one of the performances as far as I was concerned, (but too long a story to be told here). As for the latter – *Rope* – there seemed to be a hoodoo over it. It was obvious that in a Dramatic Society such as this, there were bound to be changes in the cast every now and then, as players disappeared for one reason or another (having been posted, for example, or – more often, sadly – killed or missing. Strad was after all an operational station) but this was the worst ever, and when posting came through for me our producer decided that this was it. It would in fact have been promotion but one way and another I was not sorry when he reacted as he did.* He went to see the CO who lent his support to the idea and someone else was sent instead.

Such are the quirks of fate that determine our path in life; no doubt that is why I remember *Leila Arden.* One way and another that play really was fated. We had only given two performances when Desmond, my opposite number in the play (Kenneth, he was, Kenneth Raglan) failed to return from ops., and we gave up. I hope he turned up – I never heard. He was so nice – off stage and on.

Although I had not given up hope about a possible change to a more specialised trade, I plodded on, and made the most of the summer at Strad. Of places visited from there, when off duty, Cambridge was one of my favourites, going there some-times with one or more of the others, sometimes on my own. Of my visits on my own, I remember particularly going into St John's College chapel (so well-known now for the carol service broadcast from there on Christmas Eve) – the utter contrast of the peace and the silence, and the sound of heavy bombers droning overhead something I shall never forget.

Bury St Edmunds was another 'Mecca'. It I found charming but what I associate most with Bury (as it was called) was its cherries. Bought in the market, they were quite the largest and most luscious I have ever tasted and anytime I eat cherries I am taken back there. Visits to Norwich, however, were to be of very special interest and significance.

Norwich Cathedral is of course quite magnificent, and its

---

* It was for a sergeant in change of a balloon-site outside Warrington – not exactly what I had had in mind.

many features full of interest (including the bishop's throne and splendid bosses), and seeing Edith Cavell's grave just outside is etched clearly on my mind, the particular circumstances adding poignancy to the moment in time. Her words, inscribed on the headstone had been spoken in the context of World War One; I was seeing them, reading them, in the course of the Second World War, the famous words: *I realise that patriotism is not enough. I must have no hatred or bitterness towards anyone.*

The reason Norwich was so special was because I was also visiting there a cousin whom I had not seen for years, a visit that was to lead to quite close associations over the years, and I was to see the city and its many interesting features through her eyes, not simply as a casual visitor or tourist – in addition to the Cathedral, Elm Hill, the Maddermarket Theatre, and so on.

As well as going to the three cities mentioned, I used to explore the country and villages round about the station itself – the Wickhambrook area – and especially the village churches. One was a particular favourite – Clare. When out and about with friends, I was introduced to that fine old English institution, the English village pub. On the station playing tennis was a popular pastime, and it was not unknown to wander about, in tennis clothes, with racquet, tennis apart. It was such a joy to be out of uniform for a time, especially on really hot days. Uniform was not unpleasant in average conditions but far from comfortable in extreme of heat and cold; an interesting point about WAAF uniform, it was as close as could be to the RAF uniform – the same buttons, cap badge, etc. – *and* our jackets buttoned the wrong way, as it were. In other words it was buttoned left over right in what is generally considered to be as for men, women's generally right over left. Altogether the WAAF was part of the Royal Air Force rather than a separate Service.

One of the highlights that summer was my sister's wedding, at home, in Scotland. It was always bliss to go home, to lovely hot baths, proper sheets and pillows (away from the calico sheets and wretched little straw-filled stunted-sausage-shaped pillows) as well as to a home atmosphere, but this was obviously a very special leave, and the journey north was pretty memorable too. Whatever may be said about hitch-hiking, in many instances it represented the only way to get from one place to another, and I may say incidents if not adventures associated with hitch-hiking are legion – almost a subject in itself. Two spring to mind – the beginning of my epic journey home for The Wedding, and my first visit to Norwich.

In fact the very first stage of that journey north was not dependent on it; I got a lift from Stradishall to Newmarket in a mail-van. After that I was on my own, but as luck would have it, not only was I given a lift by a huge truck going, as I hoped, to Cambridge but it was going to Birmingham, so instead of working my way by Cambridge, Peterborough (and probably Grantham, Newcastle, Carlisle) I opted to continue all the way to Birmingham and hopefully go north from there. I was delighted, until the journey wore on. It was a flat-nosed truck and I'm not sure that I wasn't sitting on the engine. Anyhow, it was the hottest day that summer, early June, and I honestly thought I was being slowly roasted alive; but it was going to save me time, and money ... Fortunately the bridesmaid's dress purchased on my behalf had a high neck – I was tomato-colour above the collar, white below!

My ride to Norwich had been quite different, but it had its moments too. Again it was only by hitch-hiking that I could have got there. Again I was given a lift of some kind to Newmarket and after a quick coffee in a delightful little olde tea-shoppe I was lucky. A fairly elderly woman in a more than elderly car stopped and offered me a lift. I accepted gratefully but soon discovered that driving was not her forte. I don't think I have ever driven with a worse. I couldn't quite make out what her job was. It was either inspection of some kind or, and this seemed more likely as time went on and she chattered away, testing out security, i.e. she would arrive somewhere and talk her way in or not as the case may be. She could of course have been quite a clever spy in the Miss Marple mould. Anyhow, off we went and after some time the conversation got around to where I was going. After I said Norwich, she said briskly, 'Oh well, I am going to Bury St Edmunds,' Knowing perfectly well that in that case she was on quite the wrong road, I said, 'Well, I think if you are going to Bury St Edmunds and I am going to Norwich, one of us is on the wrong road.' 'Oh,' she said, 'Do you think so? Well now, let's see. You're pretty sure? ... Right, we'll just stop and ask the next car to come along.' (Maps, of course, were taboo at that time; one had to memorise roads, directions, etc.)

She then promptly stopped in the middle of the road, at the approach to a bend in the road, I heard a car screech to a halt behind us, and I was the one who had to face the driver when I went to ask. However when he calmed down, he was very helpful, and not only provided her with careful, clear directions about finding her way across to the right road, but also suggested that I transfer to his car as he was heading for Norwich. I should like to be able to add that all's well that ends well, and it did in the main, but after our friend had driven off with her usual preliminaries of jumps and bumps and racing of engine, I realised that with her went my present for my cousin – nothing special, but rather nice-looking cakes from my tea-shoppe in Newmarket. I often used to wonder how long she survived her job which took her all over the country, so she told me – hence the car, which I think had probably been suggested to her as a help in her work, and no one, least of all she herself, had paused to wonder if she could drive.

Chapter Three

EVERY NOW AND THEN during that summer of 1942 I had wondered about a change – remustering it was called – and I began to focus on it seriously on one particular day. I had just inspected one of the houses in OMQ – a preliminary scout round before the formal round with the Orderly Officer (I was obviously Orderly NCO that day) – and my eye had lighted on the date on a calendar hanging on a wall. It was Friday 3 July. The next day would be the anniversary of my graduation (MA Edinburgh). I can picture the actual house now, and the back door where I stood, rather rooted to the spot. 'Yes, indeed,' I reasoned, 'someone must inspect the dustbins, test the light bulbs, not to mention plugs and cisterns ... discipline, welfare, etc. etc. etc.' but although I had to admit to myself that I had found Admin less off-putting than I expected, I did feel, as I had all along, that I would be happier and perhaps contribute more if I were to specialise in something. And so the decision was made, and wheels were set in motion, but these things take time and there was work to be done.

Acting on Orderly NCO duty had its moments too. For one thing it was an opportunity to get to know the officers. Walking round together, the atmosphere was more informal than in an office and the conversation more natural. And on one occasion I was to be grateful indeed for this degree of informality. On my preliminary round I had come across a WAAF, off duty, doing some ironing. I had for some time been meaning to iron my tie so, seizing the opportunity, I slipped it off and pressed it there and then. We talked as I did it, the minutes ticked by, and suddenly it was time to meet the Orderly Officer. Off I dashed, met her at the appointed spot, gave her a smile, a salute and a brisk 'Good-morning, Ma'am,' to receive in reply a salute acknowledgement which went into slow motion towards the end, accompanied by a look of incredulity, then a somewhat bemused smile. 'Good morning, Corporal,' she said rather slowly, 'but might you not be improperly, or should I say inadequately, dressed?' and her gaze fell to where my tie should have been. I realised immediately what had happened – I had dashed off without giving it a thought – but before I could utter a word of apology or explanation, she went on, 'I'll go on to Number 1 and see you there.' And there we met, everything in order this time, and no harm done, no more said.

This Orderly Officer/NCO business came into its own very much at just about that time. We had heard that a new officer had arrived but I had not yet met her when I reported to the room of the Officer in Charge about something or other. In there, with her, was the new arrival. I looked at her and she looked at me, and the Flight Officer looked from one to the other. It was Stella, my friend of the Gloucester roll-call, and one of these rather silly situations when no one knew quite what to do or say. Then Stella said in rather a thin voice, 'Hello ... em ... How are you getting on?' and rather meanly, but it was accompanied by a marked twinkle of the eye, I replied, 'Not as well as you, Ma'am.'

It was not original. I had heard it as the reply given to the same question put by the late King George VI to a man he had known well in their early days in the Royal Navy, on the occasion of a big review. By then the King was of the highest rank, his cadet-friend rather further down the scale. It was, according to report, greeted with delight by all present and most of all by the King himself.

Stella and I obviously just accepted the situation, and did not see a great deal of each other, but with a little connivance and cooperation we managed to be on orderly duty on the same day every now and then, and chat freely as we did the rounds. This division or marked distinction of officers vis-à-vis other ranks did not worry me — to me obvious and just one of these things — but some people used to be quite incensed about it, including one friend who was not herself in uniform but her sister was commissioned, and had been virtually from the beginning of the war. Jean as it happened was working near Gloucester when I was there on my NCO Course, and we had arranged to meet and have a meal out somewhere. Her usual haunt however where she and her sister used to go, was out of the question on this occasion because it was officers only. She was furious!

Chapter Four

FROM LATE JULY on I spent some weeks as NCO i/c on one of our satellite stations, Newmarket. A history is in process of being written including it – it had so many interesting associations: one, I believe, SOE (Special Operations Executive – contact with Underground movements in Europe – dropping agents etc.) operating from there in the early days. When I was there, it was known as 'the graveyard'. The unit was housed near the grandstand of the Rowley Mile race-course, part of which was used for the landing of aircraft likely to crash. It was ideal for the purpose – broad, flat, smooth turf – for one thing reducing the danger of fire. Sparks from hard runways were always a danger in crash-landings and especially when doing so with damaged under-carriage or indeed without one and it saved regular stations from having their runways blocked with crashed machines. It was therefore rather a grim place to be, hence its name, but nearly always they made it all right.

I remember watching the so-called belly-landing of a Flying Fortress. Most of the crew had baled out and most of the fuel had been used up or disposed of to minimise the danger of fire, and as always a fire-tender and an ambulance were poised to race to the part of the field where they came to a stop, but in this instance neither was required. Later though a mechanic was badly injured – back broken in fact – when the Fort slipped somehow while being jacked up.

Two other activities were going on there in my time, both of interest in their different ways. One was the testing of gliders and here again the conditions were ideal − no fixed runways − instead, a stretch of firm flat grass and the other research on jets. We used to hear this extraordinary sound emanating from a small hangar and it was years before I learnt that it was jet engines causing it. That and the fact that it was a German who was the chief test pilot on the glider project (Kronfeld or Von Kronfeld) meant that there was intense security always. Perhaps I should add a third activity of interest while I was there, though not quite to be compared. The Derby was run there that year − other years too possibly, but certainly in 1942.

Of personal involvements one stands out in relief! − when I found myself alone in Flying Control, totally untrained, unqualified, and what followed. As NCO Admin − sort of in charge of WAAF − I would do the rounds, and on the day in question I was calling on the WAAF on duty in what counted as Flying Control − quite a small building out on its own on the part of the airfield used by visiting aircraft, not the ones likely to 'prang'. She was pregnant − I knew that − but she had been perfectly all right up till then, and it was early days, but on this particular day she was anything but − on the verge of collapse.

If I arranged for her to be taken off somewhere, what then? But there are times when certain action has to be taken and hopefully an action will come to mind. Obviously medical help was indicated and this was organised by phone. As we waited I elicited as much as possible about instructions in the time allowed, and then I was on my own − no time to organise professional help. There was not much coming and going on this part of the unit and I just hoped for the best, but to my horror not long after, I heard the sound of a small plane, and over came a voice on the intercom, asking permission to land. Taking a deep breath, I responded as instructed, on the lines of 'Look out for other aircraft and land at your own risk.'

Whether he came to book in, as it were, or whether he was intrigued by the no doubt unorthodox communication I don't know, but in he came, found me on my own, was obviously one for the girls, and here was an opportunity not to be missed. It could be taken as quite a story in itself because when he had come in, he had looked faintly familiar and I quickly realised that I recognised him – a very well-known airman in pre-war aviation and the husband of a famous name in show-business. One way and another it was quite an experience!

Of places visited while at Newmarket, the most notable perhaps was Jack Jarvis's stables, a boy-friend of those days having got to know someone who worked there. I found it fascinating, including the club for apprentices or stable-boys, the billiards room especially because the lads were in general so short they could hardly ever play a shot in the ordinary way and they were forever hopping on and off the edge of the table, while on the look-out for the caretaker.

I learnt a lot about racing during those few weeks, mainly through an old boy who was acting as a stoker for us but was in peacetime very much involved in the world of racing. I was particularly interested in what he had to say about the rigging of results (in the smaller races, I gathered, not the big ones) and on this subject I overheard a young Australian, stationed in the vicinity but a jockey in peacetime and taking part in a race-meeting, being congratulated on coming in second in quite a prestigious race. 'Don't congratulate me on being second,' he said. 'I could have been first and got into enough trouble for being second.' Having related that, sometimes things are said as a joke so not perhaps to be taken seriously. What amused me most about out stoker friend was the way he used to shake his head sadly (and madly too – he most certainly did not approve) as he would see WAAF coming and going in a particular part of the peacetime grandstand. 'Do you know,' he would say, 'in normal times that room is more difficult to get into than the House of Lords.' It was strictly for Jockey Club members only, and certainly never women.

I have mentioned earlier how many types of accommodation I lived in in my WAAF career and I just might have added a really unique one. Our accommodation at Newmarket was mainly huts in the vicinity of the grandstand but I was told at one point that if any more were posted in, I might find myself billeted in the erstwhile Royal Box. Unfortunately it did not prove necessary in my time there!

To return to my outings with my friend Jack – two I remember in particular: One was when he had suggested that we eat out one evening – a lovely thought. I was picturing some nice little café in Newmarket (hitherto unknown territory) but in the event it was eating fish and chips out of the saddle-bags of our bicycles (Service life had nothing if not variety!) and the other was going to the local cinema. I remember nothing of the story of the film but the scenario was undoubtedly a desert island, and the music was that used now as an introduction to that delightful radio programme 'Desert Island Discs'. To an extent, depending on the subject, I am a pretty regular listener and find myself back in Newmarket. Just in case, I have my eight records lined up, including The Royal Air Force Marchpast – marching up and down the sand, recalling those unforgettable years – the people, the places, the lot.

And there was one activity in which I took part there and nowhere else – what would now be called jogging. I noted it as 'early-morning runs through the long wet grass' – I imagine dew. It was a favourite ploy of Jack's and as it happened it was to stand me in good stead – good training – because a Sports Day was looming up at our parent station Strad, and some of us were entering for as many events as possible.

That day, Sports Day, Wednesday 19 August I see from the diary, was undoubtedly one of the highlights of my whole time based at Stradishall. It was a lovely day, I remember – sunny, warm – one was out of uniform all the time (shorts and shirt), it was fun, and it provided me with one of the few photographs

Sports Day at RAF Stradishall 19 August 1942

I have of my whole WAAF career. The sack race is taking place, and among those seated by the side of the track is our CO, Group Captain Boyle, one of his small sons on his knee, his wife standing nearby (also in shorts and shirt, she took part in many of the events and was one of the best) and all cheering on the competitors. One of the officers (code and cypher, I seem to remember) and a corporal friend of mine are neck-and-neck in the lead, myself obviously struggling rather, and about fifth or sixth.

Two of the races were quite something – the final of the hurdles (women) and the obstacle race. In the former a tall, athletic figure was way out in front from the word go, positively flying over the hurdles. This was our CO's wife – Mrs Boyle – and she was probably back on the rails watching the rest of us toil over them. The other memorable race, the obstacle race, was quite the event of the day. The number of starters was legion (must have been unlimited) and off we set, a truly motley throng.

The first obstacle was a row of about six tyres dangling on ropes and to be scrambled through. The dental officer and I arrived at the same one simultaneously and neither would give way. It became a matter of principle in the end, and long after the other tyres were free, there we were, still doing battle. In the end one gave way and on we went. The rest of the field was away ahead by this time but I chased on, clearing most but my hair getting tangled up while scrambling under the pegged-down net. At last the end was in sight – only two obstacles to go. By this time there were only two of us left in the race, and my fellow-survivor was none other than the Group Captain himself. He was trying to toss ball through the netball net or goal. He was well over 6 ft. and my mere 5 ft 3 had no hope unless he dropped the ball which he didn't. At last he won through, and I won through and dashed to the final 'obstacle'. This was a row of buckets of water in which apples were floating. One had to get one in one's teeth and race with it to the finishing line. To reduce time and gap to a minimum, I plunged right in and raced, dripping, to the finishing post, to be told later that dogs had been drinking out of the buckets all afternoon!

I shall record only two other memories of Newmarket days – the Salvation Army canteen, and the first public parade in which I took part.

Just as one adapted to living conditions in service life, so one adapted to the food, though I must admit it took a bit of getting used to at first – the sweet tea, the one plate only, the mad rush to a table before the elements met, already sweetened porridge and no milk to be added – this I only ever took once when it was the only thing on offer when I was about to embark on a journey very early in the morning, Newmarket to Aberdeen, with no certainty of any food on the way. The food then was edible and adequate but I don't know what we would have done without canteens. There was the NAAFI of course, serving a useful purpose, but at Newmarket my vote went to the Salvation

Army. Many is the evening meal I had there. We used their canteen too for camp services.

While on the subject of food, I know I mentioned earlier about our 'irons' and the washing-up arrangements – those awful tubs by the cookhouse door – but I have not told the story of the mugs. As indicated they were gigantic. I often wish I had noted the diameter while I still had one in my possession, but one thing I did do was draw round it on a piece of paper which I enclosed in a letter home soon after I joined up. It featured in quite an occasion while at Strad, in the barrack-block days there, I remember, because I remember the discomfort of sitting round in a group, crouched on a lower bunk or dangling from a top one. One of the girls had got news that her fiancé who had been missing had been taken prisoner and then escaped. He had rung her up from London and had made all plans for their wedding. So off she went to London, to be married, was married and then came back to Strad for the night, to go on leave next day. (This way they would have longer – I had worked it all out very carefully!) Here she was back among us, for this one night, and with her she had brought, to celebrate, a bottle of liqueur – apricot, I seem to remember. All we had to drink out of were our issue mugs and there we sat, drinking their health, heads strained back as we waited for the liqueur to find its way to the rim, for the usual measure or tot would just have covered the bottom, and although we had a little more than that, it still had a long way to come. I may add that it was easier for me for I finished up with several people's share surreptitiously added. No one else seemed to like it. It really was quite a celebration.

Then the parade: Parades – big ones – as far as WAAF were concerned were something of a nightmare because, as the most junior section of the most junior service, we marched right at the end of the fighting services. If it were a long, public parade, with more than one band, the next band would be right behind us, and we were in the invidious position of keeping in step with those in front of us, regardless of band behind, or with it, regardless of comrades ahead. There was an added cause for anxiety as far as this Newmarket parade was concerned; it was to be my first as parade WAAF NCO. As with so many things, it looks as though there is nothing to it, but ... However, I kept telling myself, all you have to do is keep on the alert and follow the officer's commands. Then, just before we marched off, the officer half-turned and whispered, 'You'll keep me right, won't you, Corporal. This is my first parade.' I don't think I ever did tell her that it was my first too; I certainly didn't there and then. Thankfully nothing untoward happened and all went well.

Then the great day dawned: I was to report to the CO for interview in connection with my transfer, to the Met. Office. I would have preferred to have worked in a Met. Office first as an assistant, as the WAAF were called who did the hourly observations, etc. They were non-commissioned, but a degree, ideally including maths and physics, was at that time a necessary qualification for forecasters and they wanted me to go in in that capacity, which I did. It was a job that had, as it were, a commission with it and so my interview concerned transfer to the Meteorological Office and a Commission Board at the same time. All I can recall of that interview with the CO is the Group Captain's comment: 'I will recommend you for this on one condition – that you do something about our weather.' (We had had a spell of horrible weather.)

Before I leave the Admin stage of my career, however, let me say that it was a wonderful experience in many ways and particularly valuable as background for an officer, which was my next step. Many who became forecasters were so-called direct entry – from civilian life direct to Officers' Training. I was glad to have had that year in the ranks and – yes – Admin. Before I leave Stradishall, let me linger a while on some of the many friends I made there.

Chapter Four

I wonder, for instance, if the names Dibden and Benbow I see mentioned quite often in educational journals are the two I came to know in the education department. I wonder too about Rosemary and Frankie, two of my earliest friends, and Sally Bennett and Madeleine Shaw though their names will no doubt be different now; and Kathleen O'Connor, the Australian who happened to know quite well the only other Australian I knew at that time. I had thought when I first met her how silly she would think me if I asked, Australia being the size it is; and Doris who was always cheerful, always singing. Doris had been brought up in a Dr Barnado's Home and was everybody's friend. 'Thank you very much,' she would say when one invited her to spend a leave in one's home, 'but if you don't mind, I'd rather not. I'm fine so long as I don't go into a real home.' A sad comment but there was no self-pity about Doris. I just hope she married happily and made a home of her own; and Miss Furley that was, and Mrs Ford.

I will mention only two more – Audrey – MT driver, who kept us all going in the barrack block. Very short and very cheerful, she used to tell a story which she vowed was true and no doubt was. According to her, when she first volunteered to join the WAAF, she was passed all right except that she did not have enough teeth. At first sight, that does seem ridiculous; on the other hand, they could hardly take people with none and had to set a limit or standard somewhere. But the joke of it was that after she had gone to the trouble and expense of being fitted up with the necessary extras, and reported back, she found that the standard had been lowered and she would have been all right as she was before!

... And one who shall be nameless, quite simply because I cannot remember her name, but I want particularly to include her, partly for herself, an example of what can happen – and partly because it was in following up something to do with her that I stumbled on a happening I shall never forget.

A quiet, conscientious lass, she seemed an unlikely person to be in trouble, and although not to any great extent, her name did keep cropping up. When simply walking about, one did not march – arms a-swinging – but we were expected to walk fairly smartly – straight backs, heads up. Every now and then she would be seen to be slouching – no other word for it – and on this particular day I decided to call in on the section where she worked and perhaps find a reason. She was a parachute-packer and I had been there before, finding the girls all busy at the many tables spread around the room, but on this occasion the girls were gathered round, being addressed by the NCO in charge. In fact she was reading out a letter and it was from the captain of one of our aircraft which had been shot up over Germany not long before. All the crew had baled out, and all were now prisoners-of-war, and he was writing to thank those in the Parachute Section to whom they owed their lives. It is true – it was a most responsible job, and countless chaps owed their lives to them but this was the first time this had happened – they were being thanked. They had never thought anything of it – just a job of work but they were deeply moved, many in tears. Quite apart from anything else, prisoners-of-war were very restricted in the number of letters they could send, and he was sending one to them – so thoughtful and so much appreciated.

As to the packer I had hoped to see, sometimes so down and in a way remote, I was to discover that her problem was not work-related, though she would be very tired at times which wouldn't help. Before she joined up she had been at home when their house had been hit in an air-raid, on Manchester, and she had been buried for hours, her back arched over a young brother (whose life she saved). She had not been injured enough to prevent her being accepted into the service, but when she was tired, it would come over her, she said. It explained everything, and so often an explanation can lead to a solution.

Chapter Five

THE NEXT MILESTONE in my WAAF career was my interview, at Air Ministry, with a view to a commission, and admission to the Met Office. WAAF in the Met Office were in a somewhat strange position. We were obviously part of the service but the Meteorological Office was essentially civilian, and for some time – probably including then – most of the forecasters, on stations as elsewhere, were civilian. The result was sometimes we scored by having a foot in both camps, sometimes it led to quite awkward situations.

For my Commission Board I was quite prepared for the usual questions – one might say orthodox questions, also some rather technical about maths and physics if not meteorology itself. The first took me completely by surprise. 'Are you,' I was asked, 'descended from Mungo Park?'* I remember thinking for a moment, then saying, 'Not as far as I know, but we come from the same part of Scotland, and my father's family are all doctors or farmers, as his were, so maybe.' I just wasn't going to let an opportunity pass, and I didn't think Mungo would mind!

It was a week or two before the result came through, then off I went to so-called OCTU (officer-cadet training unit) in Windermere and we were housed in a large hotel right by the lake – a glorious situation.

Apart from the people I met there, my principle recollections

---

* Famous doctor, explorer, missionary: born Selkirk, Scotland, died in The Gambia 1771–1806.

of this course could come under four headings: drilling in the car park near the hotel, by the lake – more of that anon; morning break in this café or that but mainly the Chestnut Tree on the hill; afternoon lectures when it always seemed to be a desperate struggle to keep awake. No disrespect to the lecturers – just more sleep would have been welcome. Not necessarily a contributory factor, but we were in pretty crowded rooms, and back to bunk beds. This proved to be a real trial for one. A direct entry, older than most, rather shy, and who probably had only ever had a bedroom of her own, it must have been agony for her. In the event she was in a lower bunk and she used to hang blankets on all four sides while changing – like a squarish tent – while most of us just got on with it, used to privacy long gone. But we felt for her. I remember visits to the 'Persian Market' where representatives of numerous firms who made officers' uniforms each had a stall, and one wandered round and after making one's choice, becoming involved. Everyone else seemed to know exactly what she wanted, most latching on to a name evidently very well known in London. I was at a complete loss – smart city tailors not part of my world – but one name looked familiar.

Somewhere in Princes Street in Edinburgh I had seen a name (I was never involved with but somehow the name had registered) – Austin Reed – and whereas I could have 'followed the crowd', i.e. given my custom to one of the popular ones, I decided to stick to the familiar, as it were, and their representative was very funny. He told me very confidentially that their customers always got through the course so I needn't worry, the implication being that anyone who gave them his or her custom was definitely officer material! I did not tell him how I came to be there. It may seem to have been a strange arrangement, but we had to go ahead with obtaining uniform because we only had a week or so's leave at the end – not time enough to have it made from scratch. The firms just took a chance. In fact it was, I think, a fairly small percentage on the course that failed.

There was quite a number of direct-entry commission people with us, e.g. highly-qualified civilians going to do the same work in the service – one, I remember, in catering – or graduates coming into the Met Office, and they certainly had more to cope with than those of us who had been in uniform for some time – general background, knowledge of the service, drill, etc. On the other hand no doubt they had advantages on their side.

On the subject of drill, some found it dreadfully difficult, and I must describe one incident because it leads to a very funny story I was to hear later. As indicated earlier, when learning to take drill, one learns among other things on which foot to give the command.

It is in fact rather unnerving, especially when being tested. You put off and put off giving the command, desperately trying to work out which foot, and that is exactly what happened on the occasion in question. The poor wretched girl was in a terrible state, couldn't make up her mind and there we were marching farther and farther, straining our ears for her command but none coming. The one giving the commands must of course remain rooted to the spot, as a traffic policeman. On we went, and on, and the lake ahead. Being officer cadets we must, we felt, show the right spirit, obey orders to the letter, and struggling within us were the rival claims of good sense and 'England expects ...' Well, at last she produced something and we were spared the final glory!

I was telling this story some time later and an ex-army friend produced this wonderful one, on the same lines: A young officer was being tested in taking drill somewhere on the South Downs and he found himself in the same position – desperate uncertainty and the squad disappearing out of earshot. Then, as they approached the edge of the cliff, came the wonderful shout from the sergeant-major, 'For God's sake say something, man, if it's only goodbye.'

We were there over Christmas and New Year but I have no recollection of either. I do, however, remember vividly our end-of-course show. It was a pantomime-type show and in one item I was to be the fore-legs of a pantomime horse (which was to be drilled, with quite comic results, we hoped) but the hind-legs failed the course, and would be gone before the show took place. Someone else's failure too had cast gloom over a number of us, and one way and another the spirit rather went out of the whole thing. I was so disappointed – had always wanted to 'play' part of a horse and had acquired two pairs of spats as part of costume from local Doctor (uncle of old friend) but 'c'est la vie'.

At the end of the course we went our various ways, I visited my tailor's shop in Edinburgh, collected my new rig-out and set out for a short leave at home and then London. We were to be there for about three months, doing a concentrated course on the theory of meteorology, and I had booked a room in a club in Sloane Street for the duration.

I had not spent more than the odd night in London up till then and I am glad I had that spell there for, though there was not a great deal in the way of air-raids during those months, there was enough to make me appreciate just what city-dwellers had to cope with, and Londoners in particular. I say that in the full knowledge that places like Hull may have been bombed more persistently, but then London had the VIs and V2s in addition, during the summer of '44 when they were weary in the extreme – for some almost the last straw.

And yet, so many stayed on there when they could have left. They had a loyalty to London, a feeling of personal affection, a sense that they must share her lot, and I take off my hat to them. To quote an example of the Cockney spirit, from Harvey Klemmer's 'They'll never quit' (1941):

Chapter Five

A London schoolteacher reports: My children are wild little creatures, 80% of whom have been through the Battle of London up to date. But they have the Cockney air of defiance. Yesterday we came across the line, Oh to be in England. I waited for someone to go on, but no sign. Then I said, 'That is the first line of a famous poem. Do you know who wrote it?'

'Hitler,' someone shouted. There was a wild yell of joy from the whole room.

I was to hear another lovely story told by Leslie Weatherhead. He had been talking to an elderly Cockney woman who was one of those who had stayed on in London throughout the war. He had said how much he admired those who had stayed on, and how they managed he just did not know – working all day and kept awake with the bombing night after night. 'Oh well,' she had replied, 'The good book says that the Lord slumbers not neither does he sleep, and I just thought there was no point two of us staying awake ...'

I have no idea now how much we were paid but I do know that it was pretty tight, living, travelling, eating in London as a brand-new ASO. I know I dared not draw out more than a certain amount every so often, and spending had to be restrained. It was, in fact, perfectly adequate so long as there were no extra demands but these could not always be avoided as I was soon to find out. The following incident also brought it home to me that being an officer did not merely mean fulfilling a certain job as such; it also meant taking on responsibility in general.

I was travelling in a bus on my way out to Knightsbridge. It was very full and people were standing down the centre. At one point it had to pull up suddenly, all the passengers standing were thrown forward, and then backwards as it stopped. Two Canadian WAAF were among those standing and one unfortunately slipped sideways before they were thrown back and she was crushed against the back of a seat. No one else was hurt and attention was riveted on her, then on me. Anyhow, we got the bus to pull into the side and did what we could. She had gone quite blue and was obviously in acute discomfort and we feared that several ribs had had it at least. However she began to recover quite quickly – I think she had been winded badly – the three of us got off the bus which went on its way. She was still in quite a bad way, though, and my idea was to get her home as quickly as possible. I hailed the first taxi that came along, made sure that her companion knew whom to contact if necessary, gave the driver their address, paid him in advance and sent them on their way.

I mention this not to draw attention to my part in it (any officer, or fellow-WAAF for that matter, would have done the same) but as an example of what one might be called upon to do at any time. A postscript: They didn't know this, but I had to walk the rest of the way back to the club, my 'ration' for the day having gone on their taxi!

Talking of Knightsbridge – many is the time I went along Sloane Street from the Underground there, but once I did it in record time. In fact if it had been a mile, I would say that undoubtedly it was the first four-minute mile. A drunk American soldier got his eye on me in Knightsbridge station and pursued me into Sloane Street. Quite probably he was just some mother's lonesome blue-eyed boy but I did not pause to inquire. I positively flew.

A colleague and I had another quite amusing experience, this time in Piccadilly. We were walking along together when two American soldiers passed us, one each side. They then slowed down and let us pass them. This happened once or twice – obviously trying to pick us up. Suddenly one said in an urgent whisper, 'Hi, they're officers. Let's get outa here.' And they vanished. We were quite impressed that they knew the difference in uniform. Plenty of our own people didn't.

Chapter Five

My favourite story pertaining to Americans is one concerning myself, at about the same time. I was walking along the pavement, and towards me were striding two enormous American soldiers. When they reached me they threw up terrific salutes. I was somewhat taken aback but nevertheless responded with an acknowledgement and a smile. To my embarrassment the next minute two American officers overtook me. The salutes had been directed at them, not me at all. I sensed rather than saw their smiles. They probably enjoyed it thoroughly.

There were two other saluting incidents worthy of note. One took place in St James's Park. I was walking along, again by myself, when I saw approaching a squad of soldiers. I wondered, but it was too late to divert so I just hoped for the best. However, the NCO with them could not resist it and to my discomfiture gave the command 'Eyes right' as we met. This was, however, nothing compared with a similar incident, in Dumfries this time.

I had gone through all the procedure of enlistment at the Dumfries recruiting office, and I had promised to go back some day and let them know how I was getting on. This day I was doing just that again as that very new, junior officer. Anyone who knows Dumfries will appreciate the full implications of this, because the place known The Sands, stretches for miles – well at least one and a bit! I started walking at one end, the turning off for my destination the other. Now it just happened that a large inspection of army was due to take place there and soldiers were lined up in sections from end to end – at least a solid mile of them.* I caught the eye of the NCO in charge of the first lot and I saw a momentary glint. Next thing, with a face straight as straight, he gave the command and his batch

_____

* I learnt, years later, from someone involved, that in connection with the wartime Norwegian headquarters near Dumfries the King was to carry out an inspection.

sprang to attention. The next took his cue from him and so it went on, all down the line. I don't know when I have been so embarrassed for so long. We had obviously learnt about acknowledging but ... Needless to say, they enjoyed it to the full. They were early and it helped to pass the time. I did think of turning off, but would it have been chickening out, letting the side down?

Chapter Six

OUR LECTURES were held in Adastral House, Kingsway –
part of Air Ministry. I don't think this is an infringement
of security, at this distance, though it would have been at the
time. Perhaps some of my readers may have heard the famous
story of the person who stopped a passer-by in Whitehall during
the war to ask, 'Which side is Air Ministry on?' and got the
reply, 'Ours, I hope.'

The lecturers were members of the Meteorological Office and
a more patient and friendlier bunch it would be hard to imagine.
But I must confess to a flutter of increased interest when we
learnt that on such-and-such a day we were to have a lecture
by Wing-Commander X. (Such is the glamour that attaches to
uniform.) The appointed time came and in came – yes, the nicest,
kindliest man but, in civvies. We thought there had been a
mistake but no, he was a Wing-Co all right.

I was told later how this came about but will not vouch for
the validity. The RAF and Met Office worked very closely
together and, to increase liaison, the Met Office representative
at Air Ministry was given RAF rank and all that went with it,
including, of course, the uniform. Now Met types had the
reputation of being rather absent-minded (in an intellectual kind
of way) and, being no exception, our worthy Wing-Co was seen
one day walking down Kingsway in full Wing-Co's uniform but
– carpet slippers! So, politely but firmly, he was asked to
continue to have the rank and all that went with it except,
please, the uniform.

I had one particularly memorable journey to Adastral House.

I was on a bus, and as I got up and walked to the back, ready to alight at the next stop, I saw, near the back, a familiar figure – my old CO, Group-Captain Boyle. He, it turned out, was going to Adastral House too, and also got up. Our eyes met momentarily but I did not imagine for one moment that he would remember me – one of a thousand or more under his command at Strad and having been gone some months by then. I got off the bus and began to walk towards the end of Kingsway. A fine drizzle was falling and the pavements were wet, the wind was getting up and we were wrapped in horrible murky mist – London at its worst – when a tall figure loomed up at my side and a quiet voice said, 'Don't think much of your side of the bargain.' Yes – G/C Boyle, and he had remembered!*

This part of our training was very concentrated indeed – mathematics and physics basically, as weather really boils down to the net result of changing conditions of air (effect of heating, cooling, pressure, etc.). We were all pretty mathematically minded or we would not have been there, but even so, it was quite stiff. I must have found the theory of wind direction and speed challenging: when air begins to move, certain forces are brought to bear on it – movement of the earth for one, the theory explaining e.g. the circulation associated with pressure systems – anti-clockwise round a LOW, clockwise round a HIGH[†] and calculations were, on first acquaintance, quite something. Around this time my mother had said in reply to an inquiry about the family: 'All right except that at the moment they all seem to be suffering from wind in one form or another. My elder daughter is having quite a lot of trouble with her baby, mainly wind. My son is under canvas somewhere in India and in his last letter was struggling with making camp in very

---

*   See Group Captain's comment bottom p. 38, lines 24–25.
†   In the northern hemisphere, in the southern the opposite.

strong wind – probably monsoon. With the same post we had a letter from our other daughter and she seems to be having quite a time with the theory of it!'

Forecasters' training was divided into three stages: (a) the theory – at that time in London; (b) a station for about six weeks where one saw the theory applied, and learnt the practical side, the application, from working with trained forecasters; (c) a second met office where one continued training, also for about six weeks, and it was up to the met officer in charge there to pronounce on one's readiness or not to become a fully-fledged forecaster. It was a very thorough and fair arrangement for I believe the three reports were quite separate, sent in independently, so that none was prejudiced by the previous one, to avoid possible personal prejudice. If a candidate, or trainee, was not considered ready, she did another spell, and another, but in a different unit each time.

My first Met office was at RAF Silloth, Cumberland, and I owe a great deal to one of the forecasters there – Kenneth Twinn. He had all the theory at his finger-tips, and we would work things out, in fact to a much greater degree than necessary because this was being done all the time at Headquarters Met Office and the result relayed to us by teleprinter. I, however, found it fascinating and it came into its own when later on I was involved in giving lectures. For any interested, probably the most crucial thing in forecasting is determining the direction of movement of pressure systems, particularly Lows, whether or not they are going to change direction, speed up or slow down, intensify or weaken, and anyone familiar with physics will appreciate the importance and value of isentropic analysis. But that, of course, is what we were meant to be doing at this stage in our training – relating theory to practice.

We were in private billets in Silloth, and one way and another that station seemed to make little impact on me (or me on it, no doubt!). One thing, though, I do remember –

letting the side down in a kind of a way. Until WAAF officers became forecasters, the Met Officers on RAF Stations were staffed by civilians and WAAF assistants (hourly observations, relayed to HQ by teleprinter, plotting the charts, etc.) and as far as the WAAF were concerned, it was invariably a case of Christian names. Partly because we fell into this office routine and this was part of it, and partly, I think, because so many of the WAAF forecasters were direct-entry commissions and as a result not very rank-conscious, this tradition was kept up, though very much frowned on by some of the WAAF powers that be.

Something had cropped up soon after my arrival there in connection with one of our Met WAAF and the Admin officer brought me into it. Naturally she referred to her by surname, LACW–, and I was in a fearful dilemma. It was bad enough to say that I didn't know her, but infinitely worse to admit that I knew her only by her Christian name. I tried to get out of it somehow, by offering to find out, or something rather weak, but whatever I did, I definitely lost face and let the side down into the bargain.

I was at Silloth for about six weeks and from there made one of my most memorable journeys. My sister's child was to be baptised on a certain Sunday in May – please would I come and take part? I was to be on night duty before and after so there was no problem as far as being off duty was concerned but there was no form of public transport at all from Silloth to Carlisle on a Sunday. However, I said I would try but they must have someone else standing by to play my part if necessary.

In fact I got there but only just. I got as far as Carlisle in the side-car of a despatch-rider's motor-bike outfit – very unofficial and 'not done' especially as an officer. When he visited another station en route, I disembarked before the turning-in and he picked me up after. From Carlisle to Gretna I travelled in great style in a luscious limousine. An army driver was going north to collect a

VIP and picked me up on his way. Unfortunately he was turning left at Gretna but I was well on my way by then.

In Gretna, people were already going to church and my hopes were running low. Still, the baptism took place at the end of our service, I had only thirty miles to go, with luck ... and luck came along in the form of a kindly driver of a truck, the last in a convoy. Although they were not supposed to give people lifts, he was right at the end so none of the others would know, and he must have seen the desperate look in my eye. Anyhow we raced along that main road and he dropped me off – a most grateful passenger – at Beattock a small village only two miles from home and I covered the last lap in a taxi, arriving at the church with ten minutes to spare.

I had made it but I was dead beat, and added nothing to the occasion if the photos are anything to go by. As it happened, I had had to change digs on the Saturday and had only a few hours' sleep – so, I had been on night-duty Friday night, hardly slept on Saturday, been on night-duty Saturday night and this was Sunday. I hitch-hiked back that night and did another night-duty Sunday night. I was certainly worth nothing at all by Monday.

From Silloth I went to Dumfries, had about six weeks there and three things stand out in relief – (a) that I was able to go home quite often; (b) I could see something of relatives there and (c) it was there that I flew for the first time.

I had always wanted to fly and did even more so at that stage, when I was in such direct touch with aircrew. It was a Training School for Navigators. Quite apart from the experience itself, I wanted to be able to say in briefing and later in lectures, 'You probably noticed this morning how bumpy it was in such-and-such an area,' or, more directly, 'When I was up ...' Of course one could provide all that was necessary from theory but if they knew you had experienced weather conditions in the air, they were, on the whole, much more ready to listen.

It was no doubt for similar reasons that one of our Banff colleagues became a pilot. He was a clergyman but he had elected to go through a pilot's training, including ops if possible, and then when he reached a padre's rank, Squadron Leader, he would don a dog-collar once again and resume his work for the Church. There are, of course, two ways of looking at this. On the one hand, the person is trained and qualified and can fulfil a certain job that others can't. Therefore is it perhaps a waste of time and qualification doing something that others can do, without? If one knows one's subject one should be able to put it over without this sharing of experience. On the other hand, it does help. One may get through to the others much more readily. Perhaps in most cases the answer lies somewhere in between.

Having mentioned padres, may I digress to tell rather a nice story – told to me as true, and it could be. The chaplain-in-chief of the RAF, whose rank is of course of the highest, was visiting a bomber station. As he walked round a corner in the ante-room in the Officers' Mess, he tripped over the outstretched legs of a young pilot, sound asleep in a chair. The pilot wakened and as he did so, his gaze happened to rest on the dog-collar. Then his eyes dropped sleepily, fell to the visitor's wrist and started slowly up towards his elbow – ring upon ring upon ring. 'Must be God,' he murmured and went back to sleep.

My pilot on that first flight was Polish, and a very experienced pilot indeed. To fly, WAAF personnel had to get permission from the Commanding Officer himself, unless, obviously, it was part of their job, and I always remember the group-captain's reaction to my request. 'Who is the pilot?' 'Squadron leader J.' 'How many years' experience?' 'Thirteen, sir.' 'Wouldn't it be better if it was twelve or fourteen?'

Our CO was quite an unusual and colourful figure. He was Canadian – lumberjack at heart – and his favourite occupation was hauling trees about and sawing them up. There was a lovely story about an airman, who had only been on the station a day to two, coming across this figure in dungarees dragging a bit of a tree behind him, on the outskirts of the camp. 'Doing Jankers (i.e. punishment for some misdemeanour)?' he asked. The answer, if any, was not recorded. I think it was probably a case of: answer came there none.

I had another first at Dumfries – my first Met briefing, and the situation was indeed God's gift to a rather nervous and new forecaster – very easy but very spectacular. An extremely vigorous front was approaching from the west. Just ahead of it were lashing rain, a gusty, squally, SSE wind, thick cloud, some very low and scudding overhead and visibility poor. As the crews assembled for briefing it was reaching its height, and there were murmurs of, 'Oh well, had it tonight.' I knew that by 8.30 – not much over an hour – the front would have passed through, there would be no rain, no cloud, visibility unlimited and a light NW wind and 10/10 stars all night – and so it was.*

The front had maintained its speed and we watched its progress from the hourly reports from Northern Ireland, then a station near Stranraer and then over us. It had been 'a piece of cake' as forecasts go, but it made my name and my confidence blossomed. I had by then got past the stage of setting my alarm clock for significant moments such as that, or perhaps the beginning of intermittent rain (the approach of a warm front), as I did at Silloth occasionally, but I still found forecasting fascinating as I continued to do throughout. Everything is variable – temperature, humidity, pressure, wind (direction and speed) to name but a few, and after a forecast has been issued, a change in one could upset the whole thing, and a change in direction of a depression can throw it out too. It was, however, factors such as these that made it fascinating, and a challenge.

---

* For those interested, an occlusion.

Chapter Seven

MY POSTING TO BANFF came at the beginning of July and it was rather an apprehensive WAAF officer/forecaster that set out on that journey to the north-east. I had enjoyed my spell at Dumfries. There were several other home folk stationed there, I had seen more of home and family than for some time, but that was life in the services. You were just settling down, getting used to new surroundings and new people, when off you would go, to begin all over again.

How different I would have felt if I had known what I was heading for – responsibility yes, almost impossible hours at times yes, tragedy yes, but some of those fourteen months out of this world.

I must sometime go and enjoy myself in Aberdeen. It is one of those places (Birmingham is another) where I have always felt miserable. I don't hold it against them – it has nothing whatever to do with them – but I must one day establish a better association.

My first visit had been the previous year en route from Newmarket to Keith (Banffshire – NW of Aberdeen) to visit my sister and husband who was on army training there. My visit covered about seven hours – 11 p.m. to about 6 a.m. – while in the throes of acute food-poisoning, thanks to very suspect sausages at breakfast on Cambridge station. (I had had my suspicions and should have followed my instincts!) I really did think that Aberdeen was going to mark the end of my journey – that I could not continue – and indeed my earthly journey as well! The only other time I have been similarly stricken was once, years later, in New York, when I was to write, 'I was meantime completely laid out and convinced that I was going to die, and thinking solemnly that the obituary notice would look rather good: "Suddenly in New York …!"'

Two other visits to Aberdeen were rather down-beat too.

But to return to my journey to Banff: when I went to catch the train from Aberdeen to Banff, I found one or two WAAF catching the same one and we found that we were all heading for the same place – RAF Banff between Banff and Portsoy. They were really disconsolate. They were English and felt that if they went any further north, they would fall off the top – they had had no idea there was so much of Scotland already.

After changing at a small junction, we arrived at a tiny station where we had to disembark. There was one man there who looked as though he might be an official but by the time we had unloaded and organised kit-bags etc. he was disappearing along the platform – that day's train having come and departed. There were, however, two men leaning over a fence nearby so I spoke to them. The reply, or reaction, I got quite shattered me. I couldn't understand a word! And there we were, no RAF station in sight, no one else in sight. In fact as I was to discover later they would be chaps from a nearby mental hospital – totally unable to communicate – but you can imagine my moments of agony – these girls' first visit to Scotland – what an impression. Never have I been more relieved to arrive at any destination.

The station was quite new and our unit was the first to be stationed there, also it was rather far from any big town, and these two factors probably accounted to a large extent for its atmosphere. We were a community on our own, and we were a novelty as far as the neighbouring people were concerned. They were not, as in some places, fed up with people in uniform. That, plus the natural friendliness and hospitality of these Buchan folk (Buchan being that north-east tip, comprising part of Aberdeenshire and Banffshire) made it the happiest possible, and home from home.

It just happened that I was specially aware of friendliness at that time because during those first few weeks the war struck my family directly for the first time. By then, mid-'43, few families were untouched. That, and the fact that I am one of the shyer breed, made me appreciate warmth of atmosphere and that I certainly found. My fellow WAAF officers were as nice a bunch as could be found anywhere (Mollie, Moira, Robbie, to name but a few), the met office staff were of the best (Jane, Pauline, Margery and the rest) and the RAF officers an exceptionally fine crowd too.

When my thoughts turn to RAF Banff it is as though a curtain goes up and I am back there – that station that was to become for all the world like an extended family, surrounded by the friendly folk of Buchan – the field mice that took up residence in the WAAF officers' quarters; the organ that walked away; the low-flying incident of all low-flying incidents – the casualty a horse; the couple 'having it off' in the telephone exchange when a certain Orderly Officer appeared in the middle of the night; our immaculate Major (in charge of Defence) dressed up in his smart tartan trews evening after evening while many if not most of us were in battle-dress (night duty); and something I prefer to forget – that terrible expression overheard when the fire-tender and ambulance crew came back from attendance on a crashed aircraft.

Part of Flying Training Command, it was a PAFU (pilots' advanced training unit), the pilots under training (u/t) having undertaken their elementary training previously elsewhere, mainly Canada, South Africa, Rhodesia (now Zimbabwe). At this stage there was instruction on the practical side – twin-engined aircraft, mainly Oxfords, taking part in cross-countries, night flying, etc. – and in addition to the flying instruction there were obviously lectures – navigation, astronomy, meteorology in which we played a part. Add to that the usual complement of what were sometimes referred to as 'chair-borne types' – occasionally 'penguins'! – anyway non-flying – headquarters staff, equipment, catering, flying control, etc., and including WAAF in various sections, and you have a typical PAFU.

Obviously when we became embroiled in a war situation, in '39, RAF stations were built in many parts of the country – Bomber mainly in East Anglia, Lincolnshire and Yorkshire; Fighter mainly in the south-east; Coastal where indicated; Training, as mentioned, mainly overseas for the early stages, for the later stages (PAFU and OTU – Operational Training Unit) dotted about, mainly west'ish. Banff in fact was ideally placed – away from day-to-day raids, and in one of the best parts of the country weather-wise, our prevailing westerly winds coming up against one of the most mountainous regions of the west, forced up, condensation, etc., hence the rainfall levels in the west, and the east in general cooler but drier. It was built on what would have been farmland on the coast, hence the mice!

At harvest-time every year until '43 they would have headed off for shelter from all the activity taking place, but that year they found not only that their usual safe haven was harvest-free but there were huts, and for some reason they opted mainly for the WAAF officers' quarters. Obviously not a critical situation it did however cause the WAAF officer in charge to report the matter to the CO. Whether or not she hoped for some suggestions or advice if not action, I don't know, but all she got evidently was, 'Have you got enough chairs?' – the old idea of a woman on a chair on the appearance of a mouse! In fact my room was not invaded to begin with, but I proffered help, to no avail as it turned out. I had heard that the smell of a cat was enough to put them off, and I commandeered the cookhouse cat which I marched smartly round every square inch of the building, but the mice took not the slightest notice; I guess I should have made it slow march! In fact I was rewarded by having one join me not

only in my room that night but in my bed! I had felt something
tickle my neck, put up a hand to move it and felt something run
down beside me. I didn't mind too much sharing a room with a
mouse but a bed no. In case of a repeat visit I gave chase, and
after an hour or two caught it, having enticed it into a small
zip-bag on its side not done up and with crumbs inside, and
handed it, zipped up, to the stoker next morning.

Our CO's response was typical. Older than most group captains, he was affectionately known as 'Daddy Peck' and he did
have a somewhat gruff manner but not in an off-putting way.
His response to the follow-up to the aforementioned low-flying
incident was another example. When the horse had been struck,
quite a large piece of a wing had broken off, and to the adjutant's
disbelief, when the day and time approached for the pilot concerned to report to be interviewed by the CO, in the adjoining
office, he heard a strange scraping noise in the corridor outside.
Yes, in addition to the evidence, verbal and if indicated written,
which he had been instructed to bring with him, the pilot had
brought with him the large piece of wing. The adjutant's first
reaction was how ridiculous, he must leave the latter in his
office, then he thought no, and as he closed the door on them,
he heard the familiar gruff voice, 'I suppose the horse is outside.'

And something of interest about the CO personally: always
keen on flying, every now and then he would leave his desk
and head off up to the airfield. In fact I have often wondered if
perhaps that was why he was said to be one of the oldest group
captains in the Service – some even said the oldest. Did he
perhaps prefer to be in close touch with flying rather than rise
up the ranks – in teaching terms continue to teach in the
classroom? And this was not just to be around; he would go
off on a flight, and there was another side to this. He would
quite often invite someone to accompany him, and to be invited
by one's CO is akin to a command, but as it happened this was
something to be avoided at all costs. It was nothing to do with

his skill as a pilot but he could, and frequently would, fly to an extraordinarily high level without oxygen – a scary experience for some. The result was – anytime he seemed to be becoming rather restless at his desk, any and everyone took cover!

Another of the older than most became quite a frequent opposite number of mine on the table-tennis table. A room in the officer's mess was set aside for one of these and a billiards table. He had a terrific service – very low and with so much top spin that it positively curled over his opponent's end of the table so that one had to loft the ball to clear the edge – an easy kill. Naturally he was very keen but one did have a break every now and then while he went off to the bar to top up his glass: then when the result was that he was finding it difficult to follow the moving ball, we would move over to the other table, which is how I became introduced to billiards. We also had a squash court but I was familiar with it – not a particular favourite but it does have the advantage of providing a lot of exercise in a short time, quite a consideration when time off work could be severely limited – more of that in due course.

Our officer i/c Defence was however *the* character of that generation, and one particular experience with him I shall never forget – a quite extraordinary scene in the ante-room of the officers' mess one cold, very cold, winter evening. The room was heated by two stoves out in the middle of the floor, with chimneys to the ceiling (probably the standard for large huts of this nature) and when I went in, all present were grouped round both – two large solid-looking masses of humanity. Major C. must have gone in just ahead of me and he was standing back from both, on his own, aloof. I hesitated while I was still some way off, and next thing I knew, he was bowing to me, approached and began to address me in formal tones. I was to have two poems recited to me – if I remember rightly A. E. Housman's 'In valleys green and still' and 'Soldier from the war returning' – and they seemed never-ending. Having poetry recited to one is experience enough without a captive audience transfixed ...

Our gallant Major certainly stood out within for him an unusual context to say the least. Whether or not the RAF Regiment took over responsibility later, I don't know, but at that time an Army officer was in charge of defence. What it must have been like from his point of view one can only imagine. He was much too polite to cast aspersions, but there are stories galore about Royal Navy and Army thoughts about the RAF – young (formed officially in 1918 compared with their foundation centuries ago), totally lacking in tradition, etc. etc. etc. One of my favourite ones is the story told of endless criticisms having been levelled at it by members of the other Services, culminating in the throw-away line: 'Cinderella of the Services' and the rather nice rejoinder: 'But don't forget, Cinderella had two ugly sisters!'

One met so many different people in service life, and not only in the service itself. I remember meeting one of particular interest who was one of the cast in an ENSA show, at Banff. Obviously entertainment was not a must, but these shows were organised by the powers-that-be and visited outlying stations in this country and overseas. Banff evidently qualified, and their visit was greatly appreciated. As it happened I was not able to attend – on duty – but I had a most interesting conversation with a violinist in the mess earlier in the evening. Probably in her fifties, British, she lived in the Middle East, the only place, she said, where she felt at home. After war broke out, she felt that she must come back to play some part, she was a violinist (and, I was told, outstanding) and she was taken on by ENSA. But, she said, she would go back to the Middle East as soon as possible after. She was convinced that that had been her home in a former life. A year or two later I was to meet a very famous pianist, on another station – both fascinating in themselves and in the stories they had to tell.

Chapter Seven

Always church-minded (but not taken for granted – questions along the way – and very ecumenically minded – thinking of Christianity as one, as it were – one source, one text – the Bible) I always enjoyed the short, simple, interdenominational service held on Sunday mornings, and as often as not played the organ, frequently following night-duty. It was a harmonium – the bellows operated by foot-pedals – so any pianist could play, but it did have its moments, probably the most memorable as far as I was concerned, at Banff, when the organ seemed to be receding and I found myself, as I described it, playing with my fingernails! The service was held in a small hut provided for such a use – anything outwith service routine – concerts, recreation of any kind, and dances – very much dances – because that was what led to my predicament. When a dance was 'on the cards' the floor would be sprayed or sprinkled with some substance which made it slippery (so that even service shoes or boots would slide) and on this occasion it had been dealt with 'in extremis' and it was not the organ retreating but my chair. There were not many there that morning and I had been singing as well as playing and pumping away with my feet, and obviously had not noticed. I am ashamed to say that when I realised, I stopped playing and inched my chair surreptitiously forward while I looked underneath, rattled the lever operated by one's knees for volume, sat back and set off again merrily – in other words ascribing blame, hopefully, to the organ and not the organist!

Mention of church takes me back to some of the little churches in the villages round about, to two in particular to which I would go on my bicycle every now and then. I had bought a bicycle in Banff, a very wartime one, all black, explored a bit of the country round about, and every now and then visited new-found friends, notably the Turners at a nearby farm. One of my favourites was a very small fishing village close to our station, and one service in particular I shall always remember. The context – everything to do with fishing – was obviously a gift for a preacher (recalling here Wilfred Grenfell's* lovely words; 'I can understand why Christ chose so many men who went "down to the sea in ships" as the safest repositories for His truth – honest, brave, self-reliant, resourceful men, even if a bit behind in their education.') And even the size of the Sea of Galilee was given as supporting probably so many fishing boats – 40, I remember. This, I may say, was greeted with satisfied nods from the fathers of the many families present. The WAAF present worked it out afterwards and had great pleasure in recalling it when on a visit to Israel many years later.

Another occasion, another village, I also remember though for a very different reason. Normally I would park my bicycle outside and go in and sit quietly somewhere near the back. This day, however, the minister's wife had seen me come in. She was sitting at the front of one of the transepts, in full view of the rest of the church. She got up, strode down the length of the church, grabbed me by the arm and marched me up to her pew. It was done no doubt as a friendly, welcoming gesture but, knowing all too well the reputation women in uniform had (you have no idea the leaflets we were given sometimes – railway stations often) and I felt for all the world like the prodigal on return or a brand plucked from the burning.

Something else that took me off the camp every now and then, in late summer, was helping with the harvest. Obviously in wartime there can be very real shortages in manpower any-where, anytime, as men and women volunteer to serve in some wartime capacity, and it was quite usual for service personnel to help out when off duty. When at Stradishall I had been one of a number helping with fruit-picking thereabouts – that part of the country great fruit country, and some had to be picked within a

---

* Medical missionary mainly off Labrador and founded, among others, Grenfell Mission Hospital etc. in Newfoundland.

certain time – I seem to remember blackcurrants within three weeks. At Banff it was the harvest. As well as helping out, I enjoyed it to the full. What can be more pleasant than sitting dreaming, leaning on a stook, while the load is taken to the farm some distance away,* especially when the sun is shining and the view the hills of the north outlined across a Scottish firth.

It had its interesting side too. I had heard that that part of Scotland had been not exactly cut off from the rest of the country, but with its essential tradition of fishing, and countless fishing villages round the coast, it had more comings and goings with the islands – very much e.g. Shetland, and indeed Scandinavia (which came into its own very much during the war with the all-important comings and goings Shetland to and from Norway, with agents being transported in fishing-boats – Norwegian and Shetland indistinguishable – and known as 'The Shetland Bus'). Added to this, it was one of the last parts of the country to be served by a railway so that it remained relatively isolated longer that it might otherwise have been; and indeed it almost had a language of its own. Certainly when the men spoke to me direct, I could understand, but I could not always follow them when they spoke among themselves.

By now readers might be forgiven for wondering when and how our work fitted into the picture. In fact we were Training Command, and although pilots were to be trained as quickly as possible, obviously operational stations had priority, and more often than not we were short-staffed, for one spell just two of us covering 24 hours – twelve on twelve off, with 24 when changing over from days to nights, and for a time 24 on 24 off. Admittedly one was young then but ... Hesitation here but it happened and these things happened, and as in life sometimes there was a plus at the end – well, in due course.

---

* As was the custom then.

An extremely vigorous cold front was approaching from the west, and although pretty devastating when they strike, fronts like this are easy to time – judged ahead from charts, and speed monitored from the hourly reports sent in to HQ from all Stations, and sent out from there by teleprinter after the hour, in this case a careful eye on stations to our west, Stornoway etc. Ample warning had been given and all would have been well – all aircraft grounded in time – but unfortunately two aircraft from another station had been heading further up the Firth and met the front. They quickly doubled back and asked permission to land. This was while two of ours were still up. The obvious thing would have been for them to be given permission to land and for our two to be diverted to one of our satellites to the east further ahead of the front.

Unfortunately however the two concerned were under training in a unit whose officer in charge thought otherwise ... His boys could land in any conditions. No amount of warning made any difference, and we were powerless to take any decisions. We provided the information; those in charge of flying did that. As it turned out, the front reached us exactly as forecast – a horrendous squall and conditions generally. The two small light aircraft were caught up and I knew what would happen. The squadron-leader concerned was covering up, and as he prepared for the worst, comments about the problems of forecasting, 'couldn't always be exact', could be heard. If the worst happened, he could be in trouble, but if met. (i.e. the forecaster) could be blamed, well, they couldn't be exact. Our reputation counted for nothing at times like this. In the event the two made it – landed safely – albeit with, as I was told, a pint or two of fuel.

The 'plus' referred to cropped up on my next station when I was anxious to have extra equipment provided in the office and my squadron-leader-of-unhappy-memory happened to have been posted to there too, and he couldn't have been more helpful!

One or two more unusual forecasts come to mind when I

look back to those days. One was for pigeons. Obviously carrier pigeons were not used as much in the Second World War as in the First but some aircraft did carry them, and how I came into this was because the weather had clamped since a batch had arrived to be released on training. I was told that they could not be released if the cloud were below a certain level and the wind above a certain level. I don't remember visibility coming into it. The problem was, if conditions were to remain as they were for more than a certain length of time, food would have to be obtained for them, so a forecast was requested from Banff to wherever, over the following few days. I have always rather liked stories about carrier pigeons, herewith a favourite:

It was during the First World War. A crucial battle had been taking place, some distance away, and no news had been received at base HQ. Then a pigeon was to be seen approaching – great excitement and anticipation, as all concerned gathered round. It duly landed, the message was removed and unfolded and read out: 'Fed up looking after this bloody bird'!

Another concerned a most extraordinary-looking aircraft – a Walrus. It was amphibious and it had landed in our nearby river between Banff and Macduff above the bridge. Please could they have information about the tide, plus a forecast? Another was more straightforward but I was to learn something through it about Amy Mollison and her last flight – lost over the Thames Estuary and her body never found – her name is included at Runnymede, memorial for those with no known grave. I had been on duty, and one of the forecasts 'on the cards' was a route forecast to somewhere south, on the east coast. There was nothing unusual in that, but it was at a time of extensive east coast haar (sea-fog) – nothing unusual in that either – but I had been told that a passenger on the flight was a VIP. Obviously this made no difference but I was going off duty while it would still be in flight and I passed on this information to the colleague taking over – a civilian pre-war met. He took two steps back and I waited. Then, in a voice of doom and gloom, he said, 'I was on met duty when Amy Mollison was lost,' and there followed a full account of what he had gone through – the official inquiry, the lot. It was interesting as he mentioned the name of the station, and quite a lot of detail, but I could have done without it at that particular time. In fact our VIP arrived safely at his destination, and I was to learn later that it had been the Prime Minister of New Zealand, probably exploring his roots. His name was Fraser and we were not far from what one might call Fraser country.

Having alluded to it, perhaps I should just mention the middle-of-the-night visitation to the telephone exchange. I was Orderly Officer at the time, and on night-duty, and although I never normally left the office when on, it was a lovely clear night – what we called 10/10 stars and no problems ahead – and I thought I would pop out and down to the exchange. As the only WAAF officer on shifts, visits from us during the night would generally be out of the question, and I thought that perhaps a visit could be taken as recognition and appreciation of their work overnight. In fact the somewhat compromising situation that I found there left me in quite a quandary. The RAF NCO was the more senior of the two, and we had no jurisdiction over them, but I could hardly do nothing. I therefore beat a hasty retreat, found my way to a telephone, guessing that he would answer it, which he did, and just said that if I found the same situation again, I would report it to the adjutant. As I have indicated before, there was nothing if not variety in service life!

As my thoughts wander back to the met office there, in the Flying Control building on the airfield as always, I recall quite an amusing experience. We had, and were responsible for, two rooms and the job of cleaning fell to the night-duty assistant. On this occasion flying had finished, I had done all I wanted to do in preparation for handing over to the day-duty forecaster, and I was helping Pauline polish the floor in the main office.

She had swept the floor and applied the polish. I was operating the 'bumper'. Now any self-respecting bumper is quite a weight and I had my jacket off and sleeves rolled up.

I had been aware of an airman floating around but thought he was probably waiting for a message from Flying Control upstairs and paid no regard. However, when Pauline, our corporal, went out to 'do the ob' (the hourly check on visibility, cloud amount and heights, etc., sent up the Met HQ per tele-printer), he came in rather smartly and started to do a line with me, make a pass, advance, call it what you will. At first I was completely taken aback and then it dawned on me. As I was in shirt-sleeves there was no means of knowing my rank, and naturally, I suppose, he thought I was a poor downtrodden airwoman being made to do the chores and he was taking advantage of the corp's absence to make his move. Looking ahead, I imagined the poor man's discomfiture when next we met, probably when I cycled past on my way off duty, so I drew back slightly, leaned on my bumper and talked away in a friendly but rather matter-of-fact way – all just as well for it turned out he was a new member of the crash-crew who were stationed quite close to our building, and we saw quite a lot of them.

That takes me back to what I mentioned as 'that terrible expression' overheard once from one of their number. It had been a day of frequent, very squally showers coming in from the north (a cold front had gone through and this was a typical follow-up) and three of the nicest young aircrew had been in our office while waiting for one to pass over, and getting permission to take off and continue their flight to Lossiemouth. It went through and there was clear blue sky, and yes they could cope with gusty winds. In due course off they went but they were caught in a vicious updraft, stalled and went in. The so-called crash crew went to the spot, came back and were heard to say – what I may or may not delete – I can still hardly bear it, partly as I had been chatting with them just minutes before – 'a shovel job'.

To return to the episode of the downtrodden-airwoman-that-never-was, no one enjoyed it more than Pauline, and in fact we were recalling it not long ago. She and another of our met assistants had become friendly with two of our flying instructors, both Flight Lieutenants. In the RAF attention was of course paid to rank, but somehow in a human, understanding kind of way, especially perhaps on a more out-of-the-way station, and if their off-duty time happened to coincide, and they happened to be in, say, Elgin, at the same time, thanks to a co-operative/manipulative roster! I am glad to say that they became two very happily married couples, and we remained good friends after the war.

Going back to the off-duty side, dances featured every now and then, and for me one very memorable one – Christmas Eve in the officers' mess. Another WAAF officer and I had gone rather early, and as we went into the ante-room to our right was a group of five of the u/t pilots. There was a slight pause, then, seeing that no one came forward to claim us, that we were friends of everyone but no one in particular – they rallied round. They brought us each a drink – rum punch I seem to remember – one of them asked me to dance then back we went to join the others. After another rum punch, one of the others asked me and off we went, and we danced all but one of the remaining dances together. That one was claimed by the CO. 'You're not having it all your own way, McG ...,' he had said to my partner as he swept me off. And so it began.

From then on our friendship blossomed. It had not been just the rum punch and the inimitable Chrys, who during the dance had been waltzing round holding a sprig of mistletoe over the dancing couples! Just over three weeks later one of our aircraft crashed coming in to land. All were killed, one of whom was M's best friend, Bill. Four had become great friends during their elementary training in Rhodesia, two had been killed in accidents out there, and now Bill.

It is impossible to describe the atmosphere when this happens – how a strange quiet comes over the whole station – unspoken sympathy, empathy and the deepest sense of sharing, especially with those most closely involved. I don't know when I have felt more sorry for anyone than I did then for M. As well as being a close friend, Bill was one of the best – quiet, nicest possible, only son, Edinburgh. He had in fact been my first partner at that dance and I had got to know him well too. His funeral took place in Edinburgh and a few of his RAF friends attended, including – very much including – M. But life must go on, everything on the station as usual, spaces filled, but they would never be forgotten.

Although time off for both was pretty limited, we did share the odd outing, more often than not on bicycles, two of which expeditions come vividly to mind. One was on a glorious spring day, a whole day, and a day to remember and cherish, most of all that never-to-be-forgotten lunch in Aberchirder (Foggieloan to locals). It was in a small homely hotel, just the two of us and a clergyman, I think a resident. Somehow after the meal we found ourselves standing in front of the fireplace, with him between, and with a hand on each he pronounced a blessing – more meaningful than he could ever have known. The other, a week or two later, was my birthday. We had gone to a small hotel in Macduff over the river from Banff, no one else there as it happened, only our delightful young waitress who seemed to enter into the spirit of the occasion – when the wartime romance that was always so much more became the moment of celebration – and if all leave had not been cancelled (now April '44 and D-day hopefully on the horizon if not imminent) we would have been thinking about visiting each other's families.

As one might imagine, I returned to camp that evening on 'cloud nine', as they say (and rather appropriate for any associated with flying and met) but sleep or no sleep I was on duty first thing next morning, and among other things requiring attention, there was a phone call – personal – for me. It was M. He had just learnt that his overseas posting had come through, an aircraft was leaving for the south shortly and he was to go on it, on embarkation leave.

We had hoped for a day or two's grace after he came back, but in the event, due to unforeseen circumstances, it turned out to be a matter of hours. He arrived, 'cleared' (i.e. went round the various sections having a document signed that nothing was owed or outstanding) and was ready to go, again by air, all in a morning. I was on duty, and when he came in, there were three phones waiting to be answered. One was someone wanting to know the prospects for night-flying; another a route forecast to Lincolnshire; the third was the internal phone – the pressure, please, over the airfield right now. Someone was in the office too for some reason, as well as the WAAF on duty. And there we said goodbye.

From then on life went on much as usual – routine duties, briefings, the odd lecture – hours on duty depending obviously on number of us there at any one time. Naturally we did our best to make possible certain circumstances e.g. compassionate leave – crises at home, overseas postings of family, etc. – and as I remember we never failed in this respect even though at times it meant that we were desperately short-staffed. I suppose during the war the more important things do get priority – a kind of first things first – and one doesn't seem to count the hours, or indeed the pay, as in ordinary times, and the differential pay RAF and WAAF never seemed to be an issue, or indeed the matter of rank (having been told of a posting which if it had been RAF would have meant stepping up a rank but not where WAAF was concerned). As I say, we just seemed to get on with it while respecting the rules and regulations – known as KRs – King's Regulations.

By late summer 1944 the end of the war was, if not in sight, then at least hopefully around the corner and there was no longer the same need for training pilots. At this time too the Channel ports were being liberated by our advancing forces, and U-boats were operating from other ports, notably from Norway. It was decided, therefore, that our unit, No 14 PAFU should disband, and RAF Banff would be taken over by Coastal Command. It was in a most strategic position for their purpose at that time. And, for interest, the man who took over as CO was Max Aitken, son of Lord Beaverbrook.

As soon as this became known, we realised that those of us concerned particularly with flying training would be posted, and every day postings came through. A practical joke was played on me in this connection, but one which, I regret to say, I spoiled completely. A very official-looking letter was produced and delivered to me. It was notification that SO M.I. Park had been posted to Benbecula. To the vast majority that would have been tantamount to exile – might as well be St Helena – but to me it was wonderful. I had always wanted to go to the Western Isles and here it was. I don't know who felt more disappointed when the bubble burst – my jokers or I. When my real posting came through, everyone considered it a so-called plum posting – to be in charge of the met office at Cranwell. Following the establishment of the Royal Air Force, in 1918, amalgamating the Royal Naval Air Service and the Royal Flying Corps, a training college had to be set up, and in 1920 the Royal Air Force College Cranwell came into being – in Lincolnshire, near Sleaford. With my yen for the islands, like my ENSA friend who felt 'at home' in Arabia – a Bedouin perhaps in a former life – so I feel very drawn to the Outer Hebrides – once perchance a seal-woman there or thereabouts! Cranwell would certainly never have been among top choices but I shall always be glad that I went there.

Before I left Banff I had a couple of days' leave, and to my intense disappointment they included the one on which a photograph was to be taken of the 14 PAFU staff. However, there was nothing for it. I had had so little time off in the preceding months and it might be a while before I got any on a new station. This was the most suitable time, so off I had to go.

Chapter Eight

I WAS DUE AT CRANWELL one day early in September and as luck would have it, an aircraft was going south just at the right time and, yes, I could be dropped off at Cranwell. However at the last minute I was told that for some reason they would not be able to take me, so it had to be train. As it happened, the plane crashed on that trip south, near Durham, and they were all killed. I was telling this story once, in my home town, as an example of one of my nine lives gone, and one of the party exclaimed, 'Oh – and we might have had a woman's name on the War Memorial!' (I reminded her of this not long ago!)

And so I set off to catch the night train south from Aberdeen, and with me in the compartment was a character known as Ropey Joe. He had reddish hair, usually reddish eyes and nose, a droopy moustache – hence his name. In fact concealed inside was one of the kindliest people I have ever met.

We duly arrived at Aberdeen and walked along to the platform for the train, still together – not because we knew each other well, I hardly knew him at all in fact – only as a familiar figure about the place, but we had travelled together so far. We looked at the train. It was full, people were already standing in the corridors, and it was a long journey ahead. Joe (it was not his name but I knew him as that) looked at me and said, 'No. You're not going on that train. Tomorrow is a better day. Wait in that waiting-room till I come back.' In no time at all he was back, with a taxi laid on, and he took me to a hotel where he had booked a room for me by phone. Then he said, 'I'll call back and we'll go out for dinner and a flick.' He did this, took me back to the hotel and said he'd be there in the morning in time for the morning train. I don't know where he spent the night, but sure enough there he was in the morning, with taxi, and he saw me on to the train.

It was one of the greatest acts of pure kindness I have ever known, for he hardly knew me. It was also a fine example of the comradeship that existed among us – to an extent perhaps the outcome of sharing ups and downs. Anyhow bless you, Joe Craven.

In fact of course I should not have gone along with it – it would mean that I would arrive late at my destination, something that we would never normally do – but I did without demur. For one reason and another I was pretty tired, and it was just as well that I did.

The staffing situation at Cranwell was beyond belief, and without that night in Aberdeen I could have ended up all but unable to cope with what lay ahead.

As indicated, the work situation at Cranwell when I arrived, and for some time, was so awful I wonder I remember much about it. It could well have disappeared from my mind under the heading of amnesia, defined as 'the exclusion from consciousness of all events associated with painful memory'. As I remember it vividly, perhaps it was not as bad as all that! In the recent past the met office there had been staffed by met personnel but without forecasters. Forecasts were received from the area Group Headquarters and distributed. It was now to become so-called Type 2, with forecasters, and I was to be in charge.

An average office of this type would probably have, as well as forecasters, a corporal and three LACWs. During the few days before my arrival two corporals had arrived, one recently promoted and thinking that she would be *the* corporal – her big moment. The other was a corporal of very long standing who expected to be very much the NCO. The corporal who had been responsible for the office up till then, and who had done a difficult job extremely well, had no reason to suppose that she would be superseded. Next to arrive was a sergeant. Then to crown it all, in walks a forecaster, and a WAAF officer one at that. It requires little imagination to picture the scene, to appreciate the feeling that was rife, and spare a thought for the poor LACWs working away with this 'monstrous army of women' overall.

In the event it sorted itself out quite quickly. In fact the pendulum swung quite far the other way. The sergeant was posted, the two new corporals (new to Cranwell that is) were getting married soonish, and just as everything seemed to be falling back once again on to Thelma, the one who had held the fort so nobly for months, she cracked up – a near breakdown.

I remember the moment my spirits sank to zero. The three new NCOs were still milling around, and Thelma, I could see, was skating on thin ice. I had gone to see a WAAF officer about cancelling, or at least postponing, some course she had been detailed to attend. Technical personnel were rather a thorn in the flesh of the admin world, because of our hours for one thing, and getting people to go on courses could often be a problem; and here it was again. In this case it was of course on personal grounds. We couldn't let the girl go. She was in no fit state and just wouldn't do herself justice quite apart from anything else. What she needed was a spell at home, and soon.

In the end the officer saw my point and, however reluctantly, agreed to cancel it. I saw their point of view. Group had to be satisfied, and obviously were not pleased when this kind of thing came back to them. (As a matter of fact I was to become involved in a similar situation myself in due course.) But she had not conceded it at heart and the sting was in the tail. This was the moment referred to. Just as I was going, she leaned back in her chair, tapped a pencil on the desk, and said coldly and deliberately, 'It was such a happy section before you came.'

An account of my first day and what followed is worth recording because it was quite ridiculous. I was in the office all day, naturally, and was asked if I would do met briefing for night flying. I did that and was going off when the officer in charge of night flying said could I possibly cover night flying. It was then, after all, that it was more important to have someone there – more so than in daylight. It seemed reasonable so I did so. Unfortunately, however, the next morning there were other things to be done – just this and just that – and if they brought night-flying briefing forward a bit, perhaps – and so it went on.

The trouble was that news had gone round that the met office was now a forecasting unit, and all and sundry were treating it like similar ones they had known elsewhere, including one who had known me at Banff. I was even booked for lectures in no time at all. And still only one forecaster. I eventually crawled to bed, on all fours by then but still on call!

Then came the welcome news. Another forecaster was coming, and another. My spirits rose; but, when they arrived, it turned out that both were still u/t. They were embarking on their second, and hopefully last, spell of practical training – six weeks – during which they could not be on duty on their own. As a result I had the prospect of at least six weeks either on duty or on call, and having to provide a degree of training and instruction – their second spell of training being all-important.

In fact my six weeks 'grounded' as it were, were put to good use – setting up the office as for a forecasting station, including making possible the display of a chart showing the expected position of pressure systems etc. the following day, as nowadays on television. It was here that my Squadron Leader of unhappy memory from Banff, came into his own – couldn't do enough for me, an obvious but nonetheless welcome way of sort of making up! Arrangements and schedules had to be worked out for briefings and lectures. One set of lectures was quite a challenge. At that time we had among the u/t pilots quite a large number of Turks which created problems, some rather unusual.

One was the fact that Turkey was neutral so that one had to avoid the odd 'when you are on ops' type of remark; language was a real problem – their English very sketchy – and the lectures were scheduled to last for two hours at a stretch. I got round it by arriving ten minutes or so late, leaving a little early, and having a break in the middle.

The greatest problem, though, was that if some order or instruction did not find favour, it would be met with a firm 'Allah says no!' – sometimes no doubt sincerely meant, at other times a useful way out. One example comes to mind. The instructor would be beside him but the young pilot was to perform his first take-off. They had taxied out to the end of the runway – all set – when he panicked, sat back and pronounced 'Allah says no'. Undaunted, the instructor got him to taxi off the runway, and he got out and strode over to Flying control. After a pause he returned, and said in a matter-of-fact voice, 'Okay – Allah's sent through an amendment: Allah says yes'. That was no doubt a case of worth trying but it could be a problem. No matter what those in charge of flying said, or the CO, or no doubt King's Regulations, Allah had the ultimate say. They also shared the same view as the Japanese when it came to failing as a soldier. Only one was failed in my time there and in spite of precautions, he managed to commandeer a plane and went in, as they say. Funeral arrangements were unusual too – near Woking, I seem to remember, the nearest for one of the Moslem faith.

As indicated earlier, most of the early flying training took place overseas but there was a unit at Cranwell for any unusual candidates and, while I was there, this included more than one from the army, one naval officer and one quite senior RAF officer. The latter was high up in his particular branch, had been flown around a lot during the years, and just as one might pick up driving a car through having been a passenger, so he had picked up flying, and all was well until one day someone noticed that he had no wings (the stitched-on variety!) so along to Cranwell came F.F.W. to do his course and hopefully win his wings. Having asked if he could come to me for coaching in meteorology, he came regularly and often, and when he eventually took the exam and got the result, he kindly wrote to me, and one of my most treasured possessions is the book which he sent me – *Through the Overcast*, by Assen Jordanoff – with inside, a card inscribed 'To the Queen of all Weather' from Cloudy Joe – F.F.W ...

In fact I always encouraged any on the course to come into the Met Office – it was always instructive to compare the chart and the theory with the actual conditions and predictions. We had our share of teasing too: 'Why don't you have seaweed outside? – when wet, it is raining', for example, and one which I was to appreciate to the full later. One asked me if one of these little man/little woman gadgets might not help (the latter supposed to come out when fair weather to come, the other the opposite). I had on that occasion pretended to take it quite seriously and had said, 'Very much, probably, but they are much too complex for out-stations. You would only have them at Group.' To my joy when at Group later, there was one!

I had been in direct touch with Group originally with something of a plea. We had been very short of staff and the hours were beginning to tell on one or two. As indicated before, we accepted what would be considered pretty long hours, recognising and accepting that we would only be asked to go the second mile, as it were, if really necessary, but sometimes it seemed right to draw attention to the situation. The Senior Met Officer there had listened carefully but he had us both ways. When I pleaded shortage of staff, he pointed out that we were a non-operational station (I think the only one in the Group) and he was very sorry but they must have priority. When I said I quite appreciated that but may we please then cut down the work on the statistical side, he said that records had been kept at Cranwell for a very long time, it was one of the most important met stations in the country. Nevertheless he had come to see us soon after and we became good friends.

Statistics certainly did play a large part in our work. Not only did we provide, as all stations did, regular hourly details about weather, visibility, cloud amount and height, etc. but also amount of rainfall, sunshine, details about wind up to 40,000 ft. or more. The rainfall count was straightforward, the sunshine intriguing in its simplicity. It worked on the magnifying-glass principle – a narrow strip of card, marked in hours, slotted in behind a large glass globe, and as the sun strikes, so a burn appears on the strip, a day of continuous sunshine producing a continuous line of burn, a day overcast blank. Obviously this had to be on the highest building, so situated on top of the highest hangar, arrived at up a long rickety ladder – not the most popular part of the job!

The reporting of upper air speed and direction was done with the use of a balloon and theodolite. The balloon, with fixed rate of ascent, was released and followed with the aid of the theodolite and readings taken at regular intervals. These provided angle of elevation and azimuth angle, and by working it out afterwards, the required information was obtained.

We also had the means of providing details about the surface wind. An anemometer could be compared to a car's speedometer but we went one better. We had what was called an anemograph. Just as a barograph, which we also had, records barometric pressure by a continuous trace, so the anemograph records detail of surface wind. As one could imagine this was particularly tricky on a gusty day, the pen leaping up and down. On one occasion it produced a most spectacular trace – up to 87 mph and back. I knew that this was about to happen – a marked squall on a cold front, approaching as usual from the west – and as the actual recording apparatus was sited about three quarters of a mile to the west of us and connected to the office by cable this took place a split second before the squall reached us. I was watching it especially because I was afraid it might not trace it to the top in its excitement. Even in normal conditions they were known to let us down, but we did have what one might call a fail-safe arrangement hopefully to hand. How we discovered this I do not know, and we would certainly have warranted 0/10 for hygiene, but if a certain one of the girls were to apply a lick to the nib, there was no need to worry. It would run smooth and true – work like a dream. Aristocratic spit, we called it!

All this obviously added to the routine work but every now and then we would be asked to undertake something really time-consuming. One that comes to mind was the request to produce, as a percentage figure, how often a certain code figure had been used over the past five years. There were code figures for cloud amount – 10/10 if total cover, nil if total blue sky, as it were – and as this figure was included in every hourly report, it meant checking every hour's report over that time. It was obviously to decide if this particular code was used often enough to warrant continuing iis use. It was 9+, representing just a small break in cloud cover once described to me as 'just enough blue to patch a Dutchman's trousers'! In other words it was used to describe less than total cover but more than 9/10. One can imagine the time devoted to this, and I may say when I sent up the result, I gave it to four places of decimals!

Mention of the use of codes reminds me of an interesting, if somewhat surprising discovery of some available, but put to good use while at Banff. These covered the aurora borealis (northern lights) and not only one figure but several, allowing for describing different types – arcs, bands, rays, etc. – and rather a nice aside: known to the Shetlanders as 'merry dancers'! They could be even more spectacular seen from there.

Christmas that year at Cranwell, 1944, I shall never forget. Somehow Christmas tends to be a time that one associates with home and family. That year I shared it with ninety-nine children without homes and very, very few with any family. They were young, teenage, Polish cadets under training. The Polish Red Cross worker who looked after them lived in our Mess, and Jara and I had become close friends.

Poor Jara – her husband had been Polish Air Force, then with the RAF, and was missing (later presumed killed, as in fact he had been) and she had no one else in our country, and was uncertain how many, if any, of her family were still alive at home. Her boys were the saving of her, I am sure, and she must have made all the difference to them. Some had fathers serving in the forces but most were orphans. In passing, let me say that indirectly she helped a lot of us too. No matter what happened as far as we were concerned, we did have family around or, if not that, at least we were among people who talked the same language – at home to some extent.

She had made the Christmas tree, and the occasion, as Polish as she could. The tree, I remember, was all white – and I admired her as much as I have admired anyone, not only then but perhaps especially then for she carried it through with just the right touch. It reminded them of home but they did not dwell on it.

I had met a lot of Poles in Scotland in 1940/41, when a large number came to my home town following the fall of France, and I got on well with them then. At Cranwell I felt again the same sense of compassion and regard. In the face of what would appear to be impossible odds, their spirit was quite remarkable – 'unquenchable' Churchill called it in his tribute to their great leader, General Sikorski, after he was killed in a tragic accident, and at no time have I met in them bitterness or self-pity, either or both of which could so often be justified, certainly understandable. Few of our people, I feel, realise the extent of their contribution to the war effort in World War Two. Many took part in the Battle of Britain – at a crucial stage one in ten of the pilots was a Pole, and it has been said that without them the outcome could have been very different and General Anders'

Pour la patrie

(written many years later after seeing these words on the tombstone of a Polish pilot killed, while flying with the RAF, in 1944)

'Pour la patrie' it read.
So poignantly it said
It all.

For whose homeland? – not theirs;
And yet they helped us through that crucial time
By sea, on land, and in the air
How many in that thin blue line[*]
Were Poles?
One in twelve – at one point one in ten, they say –
Only with their help did we live
To fight another day,
While then, as now, their land is subject to an alien will.[†]
'Pour la patrie' – how much we owe them still.

---

[*] as the Battle of Britain pilots were sometimes called
[†] written in 1984 when sadly this still applied

army group in the Middle East and Italy, in which so many of them served, was second to none.

In addition to Jara there was quite a number of Polish personnel at Cranwell as well as the cadets, including the nicest of padres and, another good friend of mine, Tofi (short for Theophilas). He had a lovely tenor voice and had at one time been associated with the Polish Army Choir which interested me very much, my mother having been involved with it in Scotland. One of their most famous singers went on to become a member of the Covent Garden Opera Company – Marian Novakowski.

Mention of Christmas brings something else to mind. As well as churning out technical data night and day, at Christmas time our teleprinters would put out the odd poem. Someone described it as the Met Office letting its hair down! One excerpt included mention by name of our Senior Met Officer at Group – Mr Matthews – herewith. He was in fact one of the greatest names in the Met Office at the time, and although I saw but little of him, I am glad that our paths crossed. The poem is, as one might guess, based on Hiawatha.

> Then there is the puissant Matthews,
> Knowing well the times and flight plan,
> Always knows the time of take-off,
> T.O.T. and speed of climbing
> With such other subtle details
> That the others often know not.
> Wise is he with years of watching
> All the weather in the country,
> Bold and fearless yet a little
> Frightened of the smoke from westward,
> Rightly fearful of the smoke haze.

Having quoted the part appropriate to him, may I include the beginning too as it is rather nice:

In the palace of the mighty
Where they plan the operations,
Where the targets, bomb loads, tactics
Are each morning straight decided,
There is Spence the great and noble
Servant of the mighty bomb-bomb,
God of all the operations
When the sun is at its highest
High up in the southern heavens
Shining down on all the people
(Cloud amounts and type permitting) ...

And while looking for this particular relic, I found another that
I had kept – also rather nice.

They posted him off to a distant land,
The fellow who dared complain.
They took him away on a winter's day
And he never came back again.
He sailed away to the frozen north
Through icebergs gleaming white
Till the sun went down and the stars came forth
In the land of eternal night.

Chorus:

Cold and bleak, cold and bleak,
Is the land where the people go
Who dare to complain or rudely speak
Of their chief the S. Met. O.[*]

---

[*] Senior Met. Officer

Chapter Eight

When they came in sight of the hills so white
Of that land of ice and snow,
They gave him beer and a heartening cheer
Before they would let him go,
And all night long they sang this song
To an eerie and wild refrain,
Till once or twice from the cliffs of ice
Its echo was heard again:

Chorus

They put him ashore with a frugal store
Of home-made strawberry jam,
A bottle of peas and a piece of cheese,
And a couple of tins of spam,
And there he was told in that icy cold
He must daily observe the weather
For the rest of the war and a good bit more
Of his lifetime altogether.

Chorus

But there came a time in that icy clime
When the wind began to blow,
And he last was seen as he sought the screen
In that seething swirling snow,
But since that day when he lost his way
You can hear his voice again
As he softly wails through the winter gales
That eerie and wild refrain:

Cold and bleak, cold and bleak,
Is the land were the people go

Who dare to complain or who rudely speak
Of their chief the S. Met. O.

I have alluded to the teleprinters every now and then, and I
think they merit a mention of their own because not only were
they quick and efficient – the data being tapped in at one end
and received instantaneously at the other, a forebear of Fax,
but they played a most important part also as far as security
was concerned. For various reasons, including movement of the
earth, in this part of the world we have a prevailing westerly
wind, which means that our current weather conditions can be
very relevant where Germany is concerned, and thereabouts.
Radio messages could be intercepted, teleprinter not, providing
as they did what might be called inland telegraphic communication – invaluable in the circumstances.

Cranwell was very big both in area and in the number
stationed there, and it did provide wonderful facilities for what
might be called extra-mural activities. In the field of sport I
played quite a lot of squash and, for the first time in the WAAF,
hockey – WAAF only and mixed – and quite enjoyed it. As
well as being a pleasant change from work – fresh air and
exercise – it meant the odd jaunt to neighbouring units for
matches, and once we were flown as a team to play a match
against a Group Headquarters in Gloucestershire. Of added
interest on that occasion, we were flown there in three smallish
aircraft (I think Dominie Rapide) and it was the first and only
time I ever flew in formation – obviously done for fun.

There was also almost always something going on in the way
of entertainment – visiting artists and shows put on by resident
personnel, and there was any amount of talent to draw on, both
musical and dramatic. Of the former we were particularly
fortunate in having there at that time A. E. Sims, officially styled
director of Music RAF College, and Russell Green, well-known
in the Midlands, principally Birmingham. Denis Matthews had

been stationed there but had left before my day. Of plays produced when I was there were Shaw's *Pygmalion*, *I have been here before* by J. B. Priestley, and a variety show called *Lights Up* to name but a few. The name that will interest most people now is Peter Sallis, Clegg in *Last of the Summer Wine*.

Among leading artists who visited us was Harriet Cohen, then a very famous pianist. I recall her visit with great pleasure because I had such an interesting conversation with her in the Mess. I had been sleeping after night duty and wandered in to have tea at about 4 o'clock, the only WAAF around at the time. I got her tea at the same time and we sat on either side of the fire discussing all kinds of things. She was certainly a woman of spirit, and it did not surprise me that later, after an accident in which one hand was badly cut and put out of action as far as piano-playing was concerned, she did not give up as most would have done, but continued to practise and eventually found her way back to concert playing with one hand. Quite apart from the physical strain and, I imagine, the problem of balance, it must have taken a tremendous amount of courage. It is one thing to take a chance on one's way up – quite another to risk losing a reputation already of the highest – but a composer had faith and confidence in her and she rose to it. He wrote a piece for one hand, especially for her.

The only show in which I took part at Cranwell was *The Mikado*. As may be imagined, time and opportunity were not all that plentiful in my early days there but this was spring '45. I was one of the 'girls from school' – not one of the three – one of the chorus. We had, as I have indicated, a lot of talent there and the principals really were outstanding. I can't remember which if any of the others were professional but Yum-Yum certainly was, and I remember being most impressed at the speed at which she picked up the part. She had been involved in something else until very shortly before, but this is of course a characteristic or stock-in-trade of someone in the business.

When I say professional, I mean that that was her line in civilian life. She was of course a WAAF like the rest of us.

There is no doubt, in life one is always learning. This is obvious but I only realised this when taking part. With opera the conductor has three units on his hands, as it were – soloists, chorus and orchestra and if one goes wrong, he has somehow to bring all three together again. We had one nasty moment when it went slightly off the rails when one of the soloists went astray, but the conductor appealed to one section of the chorus and in some strange way they knew exactly what to do – come in with a marked entry just before or just after the point reached, and we took it up from there.

I had a personal moment of panic the first night but it passed off all right too. I had arrived straight from duty with only minutes to change. I donned my costume successfully but dealt very inadequately with my wig. The result was that when we bowed, kneeling, heads to floor as the Mikado entered, I went down all right but when I began to come up, I realised with horror that I was parting company with my wig – in fact, leaving it behind, like a bird's nest on the stage. I retrieved it but felt distinctly insecure for the rest of the scene. The last night happened to coincide with my birthday and when it was all over, speeches made, bouquets presented to the leading ladies, I went backstage, to find a most beautiful sheaf of flowers, for me, from the girls in the met office. I was very touched. Then it was a dash to the Mess to clean off make-up and on to night duty.

A long pause there.... Parts of one's life are sometimes no doubt best left in the background. On the other hand it did happen, is happening somewhere all the time, and in wartime never far away.

A week or two before that day – the last night of *The Mikado* – a horrendous dream had prepared me for the news that everyone dreads. I had written to the squadron concerned and received confirmation that yes, the pilot had been killed. His family would have been notified but I had not been in touch with them then. The letter arrived when I was on leave and had been duly sent on. Obviously life has to go on, and perhaps a dream does prepare one. On the other hand, one then inevitably resists and fights against sleep, adding rather to the situation. And that evening was the anniversary of that very special outing, our last at Banff, although we didn't know that at that time.

Sometimes it is easier to cope with a situation like that when nobody knows, sympathy perhaps bringing it to the surface. I had waited until I was back on the station before telling the family, by letter, but one person had to be told. Although only one of the chorus, I was in a position where if something had gone wrong somehow, I would have been the one of the sopranos who would have responded hopefully in some helpful way, and although I had not lost confidence, lurking in the back of my mind was the idea – supposing I found I couldn't go on, someone must be ready to take my place. So I told one of my fellow-sopranos, thinking that she would quietly just fill in if necessary. She had however told our producer, and when it was all over, bouquets presented and all that, a message was passed to me: the Flight Lieutenant wanted to see me, and there on the now-empty stage he put his arms round me and said a simple 'thank-you' – one of the most emotional moments in my whole life.

I was to discover later that they were not the only two to know, and that that wonderful bouquet of flowers had not been only for my birthday. Not long after, when on duty, something must have 'triggered it off' and I felt my control slipping. I decided to go out, and said to my colleague on duty, 'I'm just going up top for a moment.' Obviously our forecasting was all done from theory – interpretation of data on the charts, follow-up, etc. – but one could go out on to the roof of the Flying Control building where we worked, and have a look round. To my utter surprise Jean said quietly, 'Thelma and I know – just us. When that letter came, I opened it. She was on duty with

Ave atque Vale
(Based on the dream p. 90)

aint Francis was roaming the hills one night,
    Pensive and sad and slow;
Assisi high up and away to the right,
    Ancona, the sea, 'way below.

The time was November in '44,
    The sky was filled with noise
For countries were fighting, men were at war,
    Ev'ryhere boys killing boys.

Sadly he gazed at the heav'ns above,
    Starlight in deepest blue,
Thinking of God in His infinite love,
    Thinking of Calvary too.

Yet *still* they were fighting. Saint Francis stopped dead.
    Silence had come. Not a sound
Came from the plane that had passed overhead.
    It stalled, then it fell to the ground.

Il Poverello, that lover of men,
    Wept as he saw it ablaze.
'Into Thy hands,' he murmured, and then
    Opened his eyes, and his gaze

Lighted on parachutes, puffs in the sky,
    One, two, he counted, three, four.
Gently they dropped with the sough of a sigh
    Down to the valley below.

North of the river Esino they landed,
    Down on the olive-grove slopes.
Each as he freed himself looked where *he'd* landed,
    Stared at th'inferno of flame, and their hopes

Chapter Eight

Melted within them. He couldn't have made it.
      He'd held it for them to escape,
And not only that – that village, he'd spared it,
      And then it was too low, too late.

The flames they were stabbing the star-lighted sky,
      The smoke spiralled up, while below
Four men stood motionless, wondering why
      He of all men had to go.

He who stood out from all men they had known,
      He who had so much to give,
He for whom they would have died – he alone
      Knew how to lead, how to live –

Live, yes, and love so that now he had gone,
      Giving his life for his friends, *and his foe.*
Was it imagined or did one hear 'Buon,'
      Valoroso amico, addio'?

Saint Francis had summed up the scene as he saw
      The agonised eyes of the crew;
The unwonted tears, the stillness of all,
      The unspoken question, 'Why you?'

He turned toward them all, and as though tuning in
      To their innermost thoughts of despair,
He said, 'But it's sadly the way, and herein
      Lies the paradox ... seems so unfair ...

But when someone dies who has nothing to give,
      The world does not change – no good will accrue –
But now you must all make a vow, that you'll live
      For others as he died for you.'

Ave atque Vale[*]

[*] *Hail and Farewell*

me. We're so sorry,' She was second-in-command and so in charge in my absence on leave. The letter from the squadron had been addressed to me at the Met Office, but not marked personal. I had realised that it had been opened but had not given it a thought – censored perhaps en route. I went up to the roof, and a cup of strong coffee awaited my return, and no more was said; but they are two of my ex-Service friends with whom I kept in touch very much after the war.

That was early in April. A week or two later when I was walking from the Met Office to the Mess, I saw our CO walking up from the airfield, in a strangely studied way. He hailed me in his usual friendly fatherly way, and signalled that I join him. 'I want to see you,' he said, 'but I can't stop. I'll explain later. I don't know if you know,' he went on, 'but there's been a bit of a tug-of-war over you. The SFTS (the flying unit there) is being moved lock, stock and barrel to Spitalgate, and they want you to go with them. You're really i/c Met Office Cranwell and not theirs at all, but I appreciate that you work pretty closely with them – lectures and all that – and I'm afraid I've lost … 'and that was how I heard of my next move – to Spitalgate, on the hill above Grantham.

The reason he couldn't stop, and why he was walking along steadily, head bent, stop-watch in hand – for all the world like the white rabbit in Alice in Wonderland – was because the King was to visit Cranwell in a few weeks' time and he was checking the time it would take to walk from the plane. At risk of incarceration in the Tower – possible breach of confidentiality where Royals concerned, though in fact I rather think she would like it – he had been told unofficially that if the Queen (now Queen Mother) were to accompany him, a considerable amount of time was to be added to the estimate – interest in this and that, possible pauses to chat.

I saw him, Air Commodore Bryant, again, officially, before I left, and again not long after at a dance, at Cranwell, to celebrate

Chapter Eight

VE – Victory in Europe. Many, especially no doubt those with friends and relatives still involved with the war in the Far East, felt that in a way we went over the top rather with VE, but it was understandable. Several of us had been invited from Spitalgate and during a dance together he told me about the celebrations on the station after VE Day had been announced, and I must say I do not envy people in high positions at such a time. They won't want to act as wet blankets and yet they are ultimately responsible, for everything, including property. From what he told me, he had obviously been very skilful, uniform covered up, unobtrusively directing all and sundry where to find material for the inevitable bonfire, hoping to save chairs etc. – Air Ministry property. And that, I regret to say, was the last time I saw him. He collapsed while attending a show, on the station, not long after, and died shortly afterwards – a great loss in many many ways.

I went over to Cranwell every now and then, on my bicycle – we shared a lot, my bike and I – as it was only about twelve miles from Spitalgate. Sometimes they were personal visits, occasionally to be on duty in some capacity or other, and it was on one of the latter that I encountered/experienced something I had heard about but not come across while stationed there. There was a joke that Cranwell never went to war – old traditions preserved, maintained, regardless – and I was to catch a glimpse of the reasoning behind it. When I was stationed there, facilities for RAF and WAAF were totally segregated. On this occasion I was to discover that there had been changes and we then had meals in their Mess. When I went in for breakfast my first morning, there was only one other there, RAF and very senior in age and rank – and I was instantly left in no doubt that I was not exactly welcome. I sat down at a table as far removed as possible, and the next thing was his summoning a steward who came in – white-coated, formal, very old Cranwell – and in due course a very handsome oak stand

RAF Spitalgate, inside the MET office.
Left to right standing: *Cecily Craig, Joan Piper, s/o Jean Weeks.*
Seated: *s/o M.I. Park, Pamela Davey*

was placed in front of me and a copy of *The Times* thereon. It could not have been made more clear that I was not only not welcome but on no account to engage in conversation. And I could picture the scene later when he would be telling his fellow-officers – women in uniform anyway not on, and in the Royal Air Force, *and* Cranwell, *and* in this building!!

Chapter Nine

A NOTHER REASON for the joke that Cranwell never went to
war was because it had not been bombed, but in fact this
was not true throughout. Bombs were dropped, while I was
there (not claiming to have been the target!), but only a stick
of three and in fact I was lucky in that respect. It was the only
experience I had of bombs on a station, though we had German
planes circling Strad one night. I remember watching one caught
in searchlights.

We had one over Banff too, at roof-top height, and I must
say I looked pretty foolish the next day. When I went off duty
that evening, I left a forecast of rapidly deteriorating conditions,
no prospect of night-flying, though that was none of our business. We just issued a forecast of conditions and it was up to
those i/c flying to authorise it or not. Occasionally one of the
instructors might go up and have a look round, as it were, and
this particularly night I was just going off to sleep when an
aircraft screamed over, practically ripping the roof off. Next
morning I tackled Suthie, our nice Australian instructor, who
had been i/c., 'I don't mind you going up, or sending someone
up to check, but ...' 'Sorry,' he said, 'not my pigeon'. It had
been a Junkers 88 caught in the worsening conditions up the
Firth and streaking for home. His reply might have been mod-
elled on that given to a friend who lived on the outskirts of
Edinburgh when he rang up the nearest RAF Station to
complain. Two aircraft had just whizzed over their house at
roof-top height, guns blazing, and on a Sunday, he had added.
'Sorry, sir,' had come the quiet, calm reply, 'wrong number. Try

Berlin.' It had been a German being pursued by one of ours, following one of the first, if not the first raid over this country – the target having been the Forth Bridge.

The mention of raids brings back thoughts of another episode during those strange, eventful years. It was understood that work would go on as usual, and no alert sounded on camp, unless we were the actual target. In other words, an alert sounding really meant something. Having said that, there were occasions when duty was put first – two outstanding examples at Biggin Hill when it was the target during the Battle of Britain. One of the telephonists, Elspeth Henderson, remained at her post and continued to send information to HQ, bombs raining down, without which the headquarters would not have known what the situation was in that crucial sector. Another WAAF also played an all-important part in a different way at the same time. Instead of taking to a shelter, she also remained on duty, and made a mental note as far as she could of where bombs had fallen but not exploded, and when daylight came, she enlisted the help of an airman, and together they went round planting flags where indicated. Normally they would be places to be avoided; they could have gone off any minute. To these and many others we owe so much.

After that I hesitate to relate the rather ridiculous episode which came to mind. I had been on leave and arrived back at my station of the day in the middle of the night, the last part of the journey having been a five-mile walk, stations were often way off the beaten track. Just as I was dropping off to sleep, there started up that rising whine – the unmistakable sound of the air-raid warning. In seconds I had one leg out of bed and grabbed my tin hat, by which time it had stopped, but I could have sworn that I had not imagined it. It started up again and I was really on edge and wondering if I should rouse my room-mate. Then I realised – that was where it was coming from! While I was on leave, the one with whom I had shared the room had been posted, my new one was a severe asthmatic and she was wheezing away in her sleep – no doubt more affected when on a new station.

To return to Spitalgate – as well as being an ordinary station, it included a Group headquarters which added to the interest and activity, but as far as the met office was concerned our work went on much as usual, and we continued to take part in training pilots. The Turks had come with us and it was there that we played mixed hockey with them – quite a game! We had a few Iraqi, at one point quite a number of Danes, all as well as our own, but mostly at this stage Dutch boys, for at that time war had broken out between the Netherlands and Indonesia–Dutch colony now fighting for independence and we were helping to build up the Dutch Air Force. I have a very happy memory of the Dutch boys. Most of them had been in the Underground during the war years, and many had no doubt displayed heroism in varying degrees, but few would talk of it at all – partly probably because it was still too near and the strain had not worked itself out; partly perhaps modesty – the true modesty of the real hero.

One, though, did speak of it occasionally, one example herewith. One of our fighter aircraft had been hit and the pilot had baled out. This boy had been one of a group working in a field below. One of them dashed to the farmhouse nearby, the rest watched as he drifted down. Now his aircraft and his baling out had been seen by German soldiers in the vicinity, and in no time they were searching the area. They questioned these farmworkers – were they sure they hadn't seen anything: they, the Germans, were certain that he must have landed near, but all that greeted them were blank faces, and no, very sorry, couldn't help. Had they but known, among the small group – face-to-face with them – was the very man they sought. Within seconds of landing, his parachute was buried in a ditch, and he was working in the field, indistinguishable from the rest, hoe in hand and dressed in the same kind of clothes, rushed from the farm. It was an example of quick thinking and of team-work and of courage (they well knew the penalty if caught) that characterised so many of these folk in occupied countries to whom we should be for ever grateful.

As far as social activities went at Spitalgate, there was quite a flourishing dramatic group – I remember they put on Shaw's *Arms and the Man* very successfully – but I was more concerned with things musical there – choir mostly and a music appreci-ation group which flourished under a colleague. I have heard it said that maths and music often go together, and met office people seemed to bear this out. As one would guess from the description of some of our work we had to be pretty mathe-matically inclined – weather forecasting very much in the realm of maths and physics – and almost without exception we seemed to be interested in music in one form or another.

As far as sport was concerned, hockey I have already men-tioned, and I did play tennis there, the first time since Stradishall, but the game that I associate most with my time there is squash. It happened that associated with us was one of the best female squash players this country had ever produced. In fact her name, jointly with another, was associated with the main championship – similar to Davis Cup or Wightman Cup in tennis. Married by then, her husband was a Squadron Leader with us, they lived out, and I had given her the use of my room for changing. We got to know each other quite well and in fact we did play quite often. Although by no means of her standard, I recall our games with great pleasure. She was an excellent tennis player too, and I remember once passing the tennis court, when she and her husband were playing in a mixed double, hearing him say in an exasperated voice, 'This is a double, you know, not a single.' She had obviously been poaching rather a lot, as we say!

Having glanced through some of the preceding pages, I see

something mentioned but not followed up. It was on the subject of courses, and my having been a bit of a thorn in the flesh as far as Admin Cranwell was concerned – never going on a course when bidden (as we say in Scotland – somewhere between asked and ordered). It was not lack of co-operation or any idea on my part that I was indispensable. It was purely circumstantial – usually acute shortage of staff – but I remember one famous day at Cranwell. The most senior WAAF office from Group was there on a official visit, and naturally WAAF officers she had not already met during the day would be introduced to her in the evening in the Mess. I was asked, 'Please if you must be in the Mess this evening, don't come within reach so that you will have to be introduced' – only perhaps not put quite so bluntly. I think they were afraid that if my name was mentioned, she would go up in smoke. I was much amused but appreciated the situation and made myself scarce.

In fact they did get me in the end, but after the war was over, and it had its moments. It took place in Stratford-on-Avon. The theatre was obviously in full swing at the time because I have eight programmes, eight evenings, and we added to the sights of Stratford – being drilled outside the theatre. Obviously seeing women drilled anyway is enough of a spectacle, but women officers ... we must have appeared on countless screens in due course as countless photos were taken, mainly by Americans. Obviously any who had been here during the war would have counted visiting Stratford as a must before leaving, and they seemed to be everywhere.

As the summer went on, the war was still very much on in the Far East, and while one may have a horror of nuclear weapons, if that atom bomb had not been dropped on Hiroshima, on August 6, and then Nagasaki a day or two later to indicate no doubt that it had not been a one-off, it could have gone on and on, fighting island to island, and countless more lives lost – prisoners-of-war of the Japs and our forces in Burma. In the event, although the official surrender did not take place until September 12, in Singapore, hostilities had ceased in mid-August, and 15 August became known as VJ Day (Victory over Japan), and the following Sunday we held a Service of Thanksgiving in what was at Spitalgate a real chapel. By then I was on organ-duty again, and playing the organ at that service was one of my most exacting and trying experiences ever. No one was more thankful than I that the war was over, and like most I kept thanksgiving uppermost in my mind for all who had helped to make it possible. For me personally it had come those few months too late, and I did allow myself a little private mourn. As a voluntary I played 'The Celtic Lament'. I have never played it since. No matter what, music can be so evocative.

Afterwards I walked back to my room, being off duty for a few hours. I was, to use that German word *'erschöpft'* – literally scooped out, emotionally drained – and for once I just let myself go. They say that the female of the species can cope with things at the time, perhaps nature's way of protecting offspring, but can fold later. Was I going to cope? Then I thought of Jara, and all the Poles. On top of everything else for them, Churchill and Roosevelt had reached an accommodation with Stalin, in February – the Yalta Agreement. It did have safeguards, but would he honour them, or had we sold them out, as it were – Eastern Europe in general but mainly Poland? We were still at war with Japan at the time and they had had to give in to Stalin more than they would have liked, because if he had come in with the Japanese, all would have been lost.

Survivors of the concentration camps also came to mind. As well as hearing about them, and the horror associated, as our forces advanced and they were opened up, I had heard personally. A brother of a great friend had been sent for immediately we came on the first – Belsen or Buchenwald I'm not sure which – because he was a doctor and a specialist in nutrition. According to Jane he never really got over it; and my own brother – of great strength but also sensitivity – how would he have been affected by the horrors of Burma?

I remember thinking also of how some would cope in a completely different way. I can understand, and try to admire, the true pacifist – principles and all that – allowing himself to be beaten up, but could he or should he stand and watch his wife and children being beaten up? Should we have let Poland go the way of the Rhineland, Austria, Czechoslovakia, encouraging Hitler to go on and on, so that we could have gone the same way? Could people live with the knowledge that they owed their lives, and continuing life-style, to so many others – the merchant seamen who risked their lives bringing us food, and oil, and countless others in countless ways?

The next Sunday, 26th, the national Thanksgiving Service was to take place in Westminster Abbey. It just happened that I had been invited to spend that weekend with friends in London and it proved to be truly memorable in every way. As far as the service was concerned, it was a strange experience, so much so that sometimes I wondered if it had really happened or if I had dreamt it, until not long after my mother died and I looked through a bundle of letters she had kept since the war. I had known of their existence but had assumed that they were from my brother – airgraphs mainly, Middle East, India and Burma – but to my surprise some were from me, and one described that particular occasion.

After listening to the goings-on on radio, Thelma and I (Thelma of Cranwell days) decided to go to the scene. We went by Underground, and arrived outside the Abbey not long before the service was due to begin. A few people were however still going in, and we found ourselves joining on. We obviously thought that somewhere we would come across two empty seats, but as we proceeded up the aisle, not a one. Whether it was momentum or whether we couldn't face walking back in full view of pews packed to capacity, I don't know, but we went on

'You shouldn't have fought'

'You shouldn't have fought,' they say,
These young know-alls
To those of us who came through World War Two.
How can they know? Have they talked to a Jew
Who live throughout the thirties in the thrall
Of Nazi rule – the whip, the lash, the shame
Of helplessness to save their womankind
From vicious scourge and rape, and then to find
Their children branded and their house in flames?

When they have stood in Anne Frank's house
And looked
At pictures of the Belsen where she died,
Or spoken to a woman who still sees
    And smells the blood-soaked straw of Ravensbruck,
    And realise that they on us relied,
      Then let them try to say,
       'You shouldn't have fought,
       You should have let them be.'

and in due course came to where there was a cord across the aisle. Someone appeared from nowhere, unhitched the cord and ushered us on to two empty seats about five rows from the front. Obviously we had no right to be there, but no one came to claim them, so there we sat with the high and mighty – one, Thelma, a brand new ASO, the lowest commissioned rank in the WAAF, and one just next up – me. I remember thinking that if anyone noticed us, they might just think that we were sort of akin to the unknown soldier – two unknowns representing the junior ranks!

I had some months' service ahead of me still, and other happenings, but this service did, as it were, draw a line under what was to be known as the Second World War or World War Two. Again thanksgiving was uppermost in my mind, but also there an element of resolution, and I found myself thinking again of not so much a resolution, more a hope and determination which had come to me that last night of the Mikado – when waiting in the wings for a next appearance. Desperate to find a reason, justification for sacrifice, especially – as so often – of a special person, I had had the idea that one day I would write something. It would be in three parts. The first would be entitled 'In Sentimental Mood', in which emotion would have free rein, one's feelings allowed full expression. The second would be 'In Philosophic Mood' – a desperate search for meaning, justification – the third, 'In Realistic Mood', in which one would be facing up to things – understanding, accepting and getting on with life. In fact it has not taken shape – not yet!

Two other thoughts came very much to mind – looking back and looking forward.

One was those splendid lines of Stephen Spender:

Born of the sun, they travelled a short while toward the sun
  And left the vivid air signed with their honour.

And looking forward, words so meaningful but whose source I know not:

The finest memorial to the dead is service to the living.

A Pilot
who gave his life to save his crew

I know I must not grieve that he is gone,
I know I must be glad he ever was,
And grateful to have known him, and go on
And live a life the more because ... because
What he'd have given to the world has now
Been prematurely lost – that brilliant brain
And rare outstanding gifts – should we not vow
To do more, be more, make it not in vain?

      I know my life will never be the same,
      As though the sun will never shine again,
      But p'raps the sum of service in his name,
      Of extra love toward our fellow-men,
      Could far outweigh the individual loss –
      A ransom, one for many, as – the Cross.

Epilogue

A s a kind of postscript, the Battle of Britain has not featured because I was not directly involved, but somehow it seems inappropriate to recall the Second World War without at least a mention, it was such a crucial time, perhaps the most crucial – and I suppose I was indirectly affected. It was after all a major factor in my joining the WAAF. We were all inspired and in retrospect, I was to become very much involved in due course.

As it happens the man who masterminded the Battle – Air Chief Marshal Hugh Dowding – was born in my home town, and after his death in 1970 it was here that an appeal was launched, worldwide, to have him commemorated in a two-part memorial – first and foremost by endowing a bed in his name in a splendid Home for disabled ex-RAF, Sussexdown, in Sussex, and, to keep his name before the public and posterity, a memorial in his place of birth. Many of the Dowding family and of those associated with the Battle of Britain became involved and have remained so ever since. Years later, when his actual birthplace came on the market, it was acquired, and in due course, following another appeal, it was turned into a complex of sheltered-housing for ex-RAF – his father's old school, St Ninian's, becoming Dowding House. It opened in October 1988.

Unveiled in 1972 an annual service has been held at the Memorial in Moffat ever since at Battle of Britain time (Sunday before Battle of Britain Day – September 15), including Spitfire fly-past, RAF past and present, and every now and then a special guest – in the year 2000 His Royal Highness Prince Philip –

Endowment ceremony of a bed in the name of Air Chief Marshal Hugh Dowding. Left to right: M. Irene Park, Air Chief Marshal Sir Andrew Humphrey GCB, OBE, DFC, AFC (2 bars) Douglas Bader

Sussexdown, Storrington, Sussex home for disabled ex-RAF, WRAF and WAAF

Epilogue

Following the annual Commemorative Service at the Dowding Memorial Moffat 10 September 2000. Centre front: *Duke of Edinburgh with the present Lord Dowding on his immediate left*

to commemorate and give thanks for Hugh Dowding's master-minding of the Battle – preparations before in face of considerable opposition, and the directing of it at the time – saving this country from invasion and looking towards eventual victory, for which we and the whole free world were to be profoundly grateful.

PER ARDUA AD ASTRA

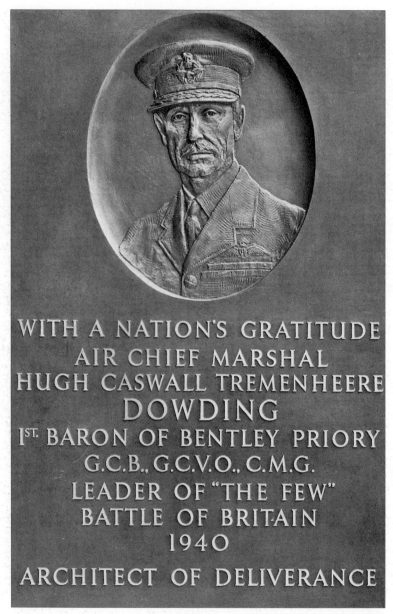

The bronze plaque on the Memorial in Moffat, Dumfriesshire where Lord Dowding was born in 1882

The Dowding Memorial, Moffat. The author having laid a wreath on the centenary of Sir Hugh Dowding's Birthday, 24 April 1982

POST-WAR REFLECTION ON '44 (CHAPTER 7)

The Voice

I hear a voice so clearly
     Behind me as I sit,
Saying, Stop rememb'ring me
     And concentrate on it.

Work hard on your anatomy,
     Forget the Hill o' Durn,
Remember where the arteries run
     And not the Boyndie Burn.

Remember it's the present you must live in,
     Not the past,
But think of me, a wee bit, now and then.

Remember when the sun goes down
     The hills across the Firth,
Remember down at Gardenstown
     Our idle carefree mirth.

Remember by the Deveron
     On the way to Rothiemay,
That lunch, our tea at Milltown
     On that memorable day.

Remember near the airfield
     The way down to the sea,

Epilogue

The ruins of Boyne Castle,
      The primroses, the tree

Where we often used to linger
      On our way down to the shore,
So many blissful hours
      That hallowed spring of '44.

Remember when we went to church
      At Boyndie, and the text
Of the sermon ...
            but for now
      It's the future you must think of
      In this world and the next ...
But think of me a wee bit now and then.'

LATER

Recall

This came to mind after reading these lines from
'The Prophet' by Kahlil Gibran;
'... and the buds of your tomorrow shall blossom in my heart
... and together we shall rejoice through all the seasons.'

They say that no one ever really dies
While someone can remember, and recall
Their life, their love, and special human ties.
But what when there is no one left at all?
Now J. is gone, am I perchance the only one
Who knew him? Must he die when I depart?
I wonder – might you sometimes look upon
His picture, and recall that noble heart,
Or p'raps upon the double picture here
Recalling a companionship supreme –
The magic moment when we met; the sheer
Pure heav'n-sent love on earth; our hopes, our dream;
E'en through the shadows and the hidden tears –
How we've rejoiced together down the years.